Urban Minority Administrators

POLITICS, POLICY, AND STYLE

Edited by
Albert K. Karnig *and*
Paula D. McClain

Foreword by Julian Bond

CONTRIBUTIONS IN POLITICAL SCIENCE, NUMBER 228

Greenwood Press
NEW YORK • WESTPORT, CONNECTICUT • LONDON

ST. PHILIP'S COLLEGE LIBRARY

Library of Congress Cataloging-in-Publication Data

Urban minority administrators : politics, policy, and style / edited by Albert K. Karnig and Paula D. McClain.
     p. cm.—(Contributions in political science, ISSN 0147–1066 ; no. 228)
     Bibliography: p.
     Includes index.
     ISBN 0–313–25852–X (lib. bdg. : alk. paper)
     1. Minority municipal officials and employees—United States.
I. Karnig, Albert K. II. McClain, Paula Denice. III. Series.
JS363.U73   1988
352'.005104'0973—dc19   88–21349

British Library Cataloguing in Publication Data is available.

Copyright © 1988 by Albert K. Karnig and Paula D. McClain

All rights reserved. No portion of this book may be reproduced, by any process or technique, without the express written consent of the publisher.

Library of Congress Catalog Card Number: 88-21349
ISBN: 0–313–25852–X
ISSN: 0147–1066

First published in 1988

Greenwood Press, Inc.
88 Post Road West, Westport, Connecticut 06881

Printed in the United States of America

The paper used in this book complies with the Permanent Paper Standard issued by the National Information Standards Organization (Z39.48–1984).

10 9 8 7 6 5 4 3 2 1

Copyright Acknowledgment

Grateful acknowledgment is given to reprint Figure 2.1, which is reprinted with permission from *Public Administration Review* © 1974 by The American Society for Public Administration, 1120 G Street, NW, Suite 500, Washington, D.C. All rights reserved.

To
Paul Crane Jacobson
Kristina Landis McClain–Jacobson
and
Marilyn Vogelaar Karnig

Contents

FOREWORD *State Senator Julian Bond (Georgia)*		ix
ACKNOWLEDGMENTS		xvii
1.	Introduction: Minority Administrators—Another Frontier *Paula D. McClain and Albert K. Karnig*	1
2.	Urban Administrators: The Politics of Role Elasticity *Lenneal J. Henderson*	15
3.	Los Angeles: Racial Diversity, Change, and Administrative Coordination *Grace Montañez Davis*	33
4.	San Diego: Managing in a Conservative Environment *Sylvester Murray*	59
5.	Seattle: Providing Health Care for an Invisible Population *JoAnn Kauffman*	75
6.	Tucson: Changing the Complexion of City Government *Joel Valdez*	91

7.	The New Sleuth: Administration in the Birthplace of the Old Confederacy *Reuben M. Greenberg*	107
8.	Phoenix: Progressive Administration in a "Wild West" Environment *Ruben B. Ortega*	131
9.	Minority Administrators: Lessons from Practice *Albert K. Karnig and Paula D. McClain*	143

SELECTED BIBLIOGRAPHY	155
INDEX	159
ABOUT THE CONTRIBUTORS	163

Foreword
Julian Bond

I was thinking on the plane flying out here this morning from Atlanta about what I read in the *New York Times* yesterday—that George Wallace would not seek reelection as governor of Alabama. The thought struck me that this put an end not only to a career, but really to an era. The public life of George Corley Wallace almost precisely parallels the birth, the growth and the maturing of minority politics in the United States, and with that growth the rise to positions of influence and power of minority administrators.

Governor Wallace took office for the first of four terms in the cradle of the Confederacy in 1963. Martin Luther King, Jr., had not yet visited Selma, Alabama, although young people from the Student Non-Violent Coordinating Committee, the kamikaze troops of the civil rights movement, had already established a beachhead there. There was then no Voting Rights Act, and the right to vote for black people in Mississippi and for brown people in Texas was still subject to the whim and caprice of officials who owed no allegiance to any minority concerned. There was then no Civil Rights Act, and any bigot could slam shut the doors of opportunity with little fear of retribution. These doors are open now, and your right to participate in choosing our government is now secure. These rights were won, really, because of the leadership of George Wallace's then arch enemy, the late Dr. Martin Luther King.

The *Times* reported, oddly enough, that by this year, by 1986, Governor Wallace had become responsible for the integration of his state's bureaucracy and the appointment of hundreds of blacks in Alabama to all sorts of boards and commissions. He did so, one may safely assume, because of the changing political climate which helped change his opinions about things and also helped sweep many of you into positions you now hold. This climate changed because of the changing American preoccupation with and perception of race, a relatively recent phenomenon in the United States. Indeed, it's only in the relatively recent past that the people of this country began to take any kind of aggressive step—and then only at the insistence of victims who were trying to inhibit and diminish the white supremist impulse in the American character.

It was only forty years ago that the Swedish sociologist, Gunnar Myrdal, released his classic study, *An American Dilemma*, in which he issued a challenge to Americans to try to match their promises with their practices. It was only thirty-two years ago that the United States Supreme Court declared segregation in the public schools illegal in the case of *Brown* vs. *Board of Education*. A year after *Brown*, a middle-aged department store seamstress in Montgomery, Alabama, refused to give up her seat on a city bus so a white man could sit down. Five years after Montgomery, four black young men—college students in Greensboro, North Carolina—refused to give up their seats at a dime store lunch counter which had been reserved for whites. These small acts of passive resistance to American apartheid, and the cumulative acts of tens of thousands more, helped create a people's movement in the southern United States which eliminated segregation in that region in less than a decade and gave an impetus and support to minority political development in the rest of the United States as never before.

Now there are those Americans who declare today that yesterday's movement went too far. These people have either forgotten or never knew what yesterday was really like. Let me let the words of the late Martin Luther King, Jr., try to put you back in that place not quite a generation ago to the white clergyman in Birmingham who could not understand why King was an inmate in their jail. He wrote:

> When you've seen vicious mobs lynch your mothers and fathers at will, and drown your sisters and brothers at whim, when you've seen hate-filled policemen curse, kick and even kill your black brothers and sisters, when you see the vast majority of your twenty million Negro brothers and sisters smothering in an airtight cage of poverty in the midst of an affluent society, when you suddenly find your tongue twisted and your speech stammering as you seek to explain to your six-year-old daughter why she can't go to the public amusement park that's just been advertised on television, and see tears welling up in her eyes when she is told Fun Town is closed to colored children, see ominous clouds of inferiority beginning to form in her little mental sky, and see her beginning to distort her personality by developing an unconscious bitterness toward white people. When you have to concoct an answer for a five-year-old son who is

FOREWORD

asking, 'Daddy, why do white people treat colored people so mean?', when you are humiliated day in and day out by signs reading, 'whites and colored,' when your first name becomes 'boy' and your last name becomes 'John,' when your wife and mother are never given the respected title 'Mrs.,' when you are harried by day and haunted by night living constantly on tiptoe stance, never quite knowing what to expect next, plagued by inner fears and outer resentments, when you are forever fighting a degenerating sense of nobodiness, then you will understand.

We ought to take some time today to understand, to try if we may to measure distances travelled as well as distances yet to come. Mrs. Rosa Parks' movement in Montgomery helped introduce us to this then new leader, this minister born Michael Luther King. He reluctantly accepted the stewardship of Montgomery's movement against segregated bus seating, and his eloquent voice soon propelled him in the leadership of a growing national movement, a position he held until his murder in 1968. He surely was the premier figure in the twentieth-century struggle for economic and political justice. When Martin Luther King was born, our world was nearly as rigidly segregated, both by custom and by law, as is South Africa today. But among this man's marvelous contributions were to give eloquent voice to the aspirations of minority Americans and to give life to a method of mass participation for equal rights so that everyone—every man, every woman, student, housewife, minister—everyone could become an agent of their own deliverance. This modern movement has passed through a series of climaxes. These were years of great legal struggles in the courts—complemented by extralegal struggles in the streets. In this period, gains were won at lunch counters, at movie theaters, at polling places, at bus stations; and the fabric of legal segregation in the United States began to come undone. What had begun as a movement for elemental civil rights has now largely become a political and an economic movement, and black and brown men and women are today winning public office and power in numbers we only dreamed of before. But despite an impressive increase in the number of nonwhite people holding office, despite the ability we now have to sit, eat, ride, and vote in places which used to bar their faces, in a very real way in 1986, we find our condition unchanged.

A quick look at all these statistics which measure how well or how poorly a group of people are doing. The figures which measure infant mortality, median family income, and life expectancy demonstrate clearly that while our general condition has improved a great deal, our relative condition has actually managed to get worse. It is almost as if we were climbing a molasses mountain dressed in snowshoes, while others ride a relatively rapid ski lift to the top. Now the ski slopes are more treacherous, the molasses melting into mud, a sargasso sea of joblessness for many, and hopelessness for many more. These classic battles waged in the decade of the 1960s were carried forward with great success against state-sanctioned segregation and succeeded, to the extent that they did, both because the victims became their own best champions and because they found a sympathetic ear in the national body politic. But as these demands became more insistent, as a foreign war began to drain our treasury and young manhood, as our best and our brightest were beaten down by bullets, a radical shift began to occur in the national consciousness. My remarks really ought to be called a "Tale and a Half of Two Decades," for that is roughly the period of the beginning until today of the development and the growth in large numbers of different faces holding public office and running impressive public programs.

I want to talk primarily about the future, but to do so, I must try to talk about the past; and to do that, I must try to do something difficult for a politician, to talk with two voices: first, as a contemporary fellow passenger on what promises to be a tough and frustrating trip toward the twenty-first century, and second, as a witness and participant to an earlier leg on that journey, a trip that has taken us from Selma to Saigon to Soweto; from Bull Connor to Allan Bakke; from James Earl Ray to Bernard Goetz; from the old George Wallace to the new Ronald Reagan; from Lincoln Perry—Lincoln Perry is the actor who died last year who used to play a character called Step-an'-Fetchit—we've come from Lincoln Perry to Clarence Pendleton; we've come from the Ku Klux Klan to the Neo-Nazis and the Posse Comitatas; we've come from *Brown* vs. *the Board of Education* to *Grove City College* vs. *Bell;* and we've come from a president, born in Texas, who had the courage to stand up for civil rights, to a president, born in the land of Lincoln, who has opposed every piece of civil rights legislation put forward in the last half of the twentieth century. If we go forward any faster it may be hazardous to our health!

Think back with me, those of you who can, just twenty-five short years ago. 1961 was a presidential inaugural year. A tired old general was mustering out a listless Republican administration and a vigorous cold war liberal was preparing to lead the nation toward a new frontier. The inaugural speech of John F. Kennedy in January of 1961 featured some of the more memorable pieces of presidential rhetoric in recent years. It was, as they say, a well-crafted speech, its ideas marshalled for maximum emotional effect, its phrasing most articulate, and its cadences rolled with measured eloquence. It was at the same time a most dangerous speech, for if it glistened with idealism it also bristled with challenge. Whatever else it did, it somehow managed to capture the imagination of millions of Americans and helped to define the political motive and the moral outline for several decades to come.

FOREWORD

One or two of you may remember with me that president promising to go anywhere, to bear any burden, to fight any foe in defense of freedom. That promise, translated into public policy, produced the quicksand of Vietnam. But he also pronounced a clear call to dedication and sacrifice, to the idealism of young and old, black and white Americans. That call, translated into public policy, produced the Peace Corps and domestic social programs for the poor. At the same time, in the late 1950s and early 1960s, something else had begun to bud and blossom as black America began to revive its then dormant revolution. We had borne our share and more of wartime burdens and demanded a share of the precious and prosperous peace. In Montgomery thirty years ago this past December 5, a small black woman did just that. Remember if you will that nonviolent protest was nearly the only available means of expression to what was then a largely voteless people. The year Mrs. Parks was arrested, only 3 percent of eligible blacks in Mississippi were permitted to vote and twenty-eight counties in the South with black populations of 80 percent or greater had not one single black registered voter, although several had more registered whites than there were whites eligible to vote. But these protests of yesterday did force the elimination of racial barriers from places of public accommodation and from the political process—and did so almost entirely because of the willingness of young and old Americans to adopt the twin disciplines of nonviolence and hard work. But since that period of great involvement, great activity, and great forward progress, some serious setbacks have happened to us all.

The sun set on the decade of the 1960s and rose to illuminate the new Nixon era. A national negative mindset quickly became crystal clear. Idealism and vigor were replaced with cynicism and narcissism. Our young people abandoned the war against racism and colonialism and turned inward toward examination of their id. As the 1960s ended, a major portion of the population had ended all connection with the struggle for equal rights and racial justice in America. The "me" generation had homesteaded the new frontier. The 1970s which followed was a decade of reaction and self-indulgent retreat from responsibility. In Washington, the Great Society was replaced with malignant neglect. A kind of lifeboat ethics sailed into the national consciousness: the notion that we are all passengers on a kind of global *Titanic*, a sinking ship without lifeboats enough to go around. Quite naturally, those who were first pushed out of the lifeboats constitute that increasing portion of our population which is quickly becoming absolutely irrelevant to the productive process—the uneducated young and the useless aged and many of those whose skins are dark. But luckily by 1975, the architect of avarice as social policy had been disgraced, dismissed from power, and a carefree caretaker installed in his stead.

In 1976 we went to the polls in record numbers to elect a man who clearly knew the words to our hymns. In less than a year we wondered if he had ever known the numbers on our paychecks. But sad to say, he lost office in 1980 and then four years later, in November 1984, the people, in their infinite wisdom, spoke again. They reinstalled the evil empire, and reelected an amiable incompetent who clearly intends to take the federal government entirely out of the business of enforcing equal opportunity in the United States. They intend to eliminate affirmative action for minorities and for women. They intend, in fact, to erase the laws and programs written in blood and sweat in the twenty-five years since Martin Luther King, Jr., was the premier figure in the freedom movement.

As was true more than one hundred years ago, a president, desperate for power, has entered into an illicit arrangement, not just with the unreconstructed South, but with the national unreconstructed mentality that believed then, as it does now, that private profit and public arrogance could be pursued at the expense of the people living on the economic edge. A constituency of the comfortable, the callous, and the smug has been recruited to form solid ranks against the forgotten. For the last several years, we have suffered under a form of triage economics which has produced the first increases in American infant mortality rate in twenty years and pushed thousands of Americans, both poor and working poor, deeper and deeper into poverty.

By August of 1985, the Census Bureau reported that the number of people living in poverty had increased over the previous four years by more than nine million, the largest increase since these statistics were first collected over twenty years ago. Three million children have fallen into poverty over the last four years. Today, the poorest two-fifths of our population receives a smaller share of the national income and the richest two-fifths a larger share than at any time since 1947. Equally frightening is the danger we all face from an escalated arms race and from increased American interference in the lives of our neighbors in this hemisphere and in other countries around the globe. What's so frightening about diminished life chances among minority Americans here at home and the heightened chance of the loss of all human life worldwide is not that so many of our fellow citizens aren't aware, but that so many are aware and simply do not care. Recreating that care and rebuilding that old multiracial coalition of conscience, Dr. King's lead ought to be first priority for all of us over the next several years.

If the years which went before—the Kennedy, the Johnson, the Carter years—taught us any lessons at all, it ought to have been that government, under militant and concerted pressure, would move, slowly and rather ponderously—all too often with all deliberate *lack* of speed—to become a limited partner of sorts with the American underclass in their struggle to do better for themselves. We ought to all remember that the benefits of yesterday's civil rights movements largely accrued to those who stood poised, ready to enter the doors of opportunity.

There are large portions of our population untouched by Affirmative Action, untouched by the civil rights laws of the 1960s, untouched by the great debates about goals and quotas today. That is partially true because we have forgotten one of the great messages Martin Luther King left us years before. We tend in reminiscence to focus, as well we might, on his devotion to Gandhian nonviolence, and how, in his hands, passive resistance became militant aggression against American apartheid. Or we remember his insistence that the fruits of his labors ought be shared by all Americans—black, brown, *and* white—and his demand that the troops of his army ought be integrated, too. But we seem to have forgotten the simplest of messages he brought us in Montgomery, Albany, Selma, Birmingham, and even in Memphis the evening before his death. That message was not original with King, but few leadership figures in the struggle for human rights have expresed it so well before or since. For him, it began when Mrs. Parks refused to stand up on that bus. Until that moment, most Americans were little more than eager bystanders at the side of a large stage upon which the drama of human liberation was acted out. The actors were those lawyers who could litigate this problem or social scientists who might codify and chart and graph the dimensions of the terror of racial superiority. The average man or woman found participation limited largely to voting, where voting was permitted, or to making a meager contribution in cash or kind to the work of a small band of civil rights professionals. But when Mrs. Parks refused to stand up and when Martin Luther King stood up to preach, mass participation came to the movement for civil rights. That kind of mass participation is badly needed in today's movement as well.

The lesson of yesterday's civil rights movement all over the southern tier of states of the United States, from Texas to Tennessee, is that we tend to move forward fastest when we move forward together. This is a struggle too important to be left to leadership figures alone. Fortunately, there is ample opportunity for us all. There are a host of organizations dedicated to making Dr. King's dream come true. There are candidates who need help to win office, like me. There are officeholders who ought to be defeated. There are school children who need special help and a host of others who cry out daily for assistance. There is a great world out there waiting to be won. The year Dr. King was shot down on the balcony of the Lorraine Motel in Memphis, the National Advisory Commission on Civil Disorder reported there were two societies in America, one largely black and poor, one largely white and affluent, drifting further and further apart. These last few years have widened the gap between those who have and those who don't and have hastened the necessity for aggressive political action against those who want to destroy that dream and replace it with their nightmare. Unfortunately, there is no utopia immediately ahead. There are no detailed blueprints or complicated road maps to the future, but if we may focus our politics on the real issues—on power, on health, on human need—we may move forward toward a more humane society. To look backward at an imaginary ancient golden age is to surrender our futures to private greed, to increasing concentrations of wealth and power, to the continuing economic crisis to which the unchecked race for profit submits us all. Holding on to victories won but twenty short years ago requires that no method and no means ought to be discounted. A people in extreme can't afford to turn their backs on any tool which may produce the motor for doing right. Doing right, after all, is what this life is all about.

Let me leave you with some favorite words of mine from the past, from the late scholar W.E.B. Du Bois who put down on paper almost a century ago an anecdote of what he saw about him then and which, sad to say, we still see about us today. He said then,

I believe in God, who made of blood all the nations that dwell on the earth. I believe we all—black, brown, or white—are brothers, varying through time and opportunity in form, and gift and feature, but differing in no essential particular. Alike in soul, and in the possibility of infinite development. I believe in service—humble, reverent service, from the blackening of boots to the whitening of souls, for work is heaven, idleness hell, and wages the well done of the Master that summoned all them that labor unto heavy-laden, making no distinction between the black sweating cotton hands of Georgia and the first families of Virginia, since all distinction not based on deed is devilish, and not divine. I believe in liberty for us all. The space to stretch our arms and our souls, the right to breathe, the right to vote, the freedom to choose our friends, to ride the railroad, uncursed by color, thinking, hoping, dreaming, working as we will, in a kingdom of God and love.

Acknowledgments

We would like to thank a variety of individuals without whom this volume would not have been possible. We are indebted to the former director of the School of Public Affairs of Arizona State University, John S. Hall, for securing the funding for the Minority Administrators Conference, which led to this endeavor. We would like to thank the contributors for their enthusiasm for the project and patience with our editing and structuring of their thoughts. Our graduate assistants, Jennie Gorrell and Judith A. M. Brodsky, worked tirelessly during the conference and only through their efforts were we able to succeed. The staff in ASU's College of Public Programs' Auxiliary Resource Center transcribed the hours of tapes from the administrators' sessions. Finally, we owe the largest debt to Marian Buckley for word processing this manuscript—and keeping a smile throughout the arduous editing and revision process.

1

Introduction: Minority Administrators—Another Frontier

Paula D. McClain and Albert K. Karnig

American history has been marked by intense and painful racism. To greater or lesser extent, all new groups have been objects of discrimination—including white ethnics such as the Irish, Italians, Poles, and Jews. However, three groups have been particular targets of racism and racist policies in the United States. And each of these groups—Indians, blacks, and Hispanics—was here long before the tide of white ethnics swept onto American shores. Indeed, Indians were the aboriginal people of the North American continent; Hispanics, at least the largest group, Mexican Americans in the Southwest, were the early settlers of the land between Texas and California; and blacks were brought as slaves over a century before American independence and through the years leading to the Civil War. It would be foolish to believe that racism has been conquered; there is too much evidence to contradict such a conclusion. Nonetheless, it would be naive to believe that racism and the formal policies that supported it have not been muted and changed in crucial ways. In particular, the three decades preceding the 1980s witnessed considerable minority mobilization and political activity, which resulted in fundamental—if incomplete—changes in the fabric of American society.

MINORITY MOBILIZATION

As Julian Bond eloquently suggests, the roots of racial change stem from a profoundly successful mass movement which began to gather steam in the 1950s. The continual struggle for civil and human rights by black Americans erupted in a series of individual, yet connected, protest events which marked the beginning of this phase of the civil rights movement. During the 1960s, these independent and individual actions coalesced into a broadly based national civil rights movement, as Dr. Martin Luther King, Jr., emerged as the symbol of the national cause. The movement used a variety of tactics to address the issues of segregation in public accommodations, voting rights, job discrimination, and myriad forms of discrimination. In addition to electoral participation, where it was permitted, there was also protest in mass demonstrations, economic boycotts, lunch counter sit-ins, attempts to register to vote, and the Freedom Rides.

The movement was clearly involved in an agenda-setting process. The activities fit what Cobb et al. refer to as the "outside initiative model," that is, a process through which issues arise and grievances are articulated by individuals outside the formal governmental structure.[1] By generating attention and continuously exposing critical issues to the general population, the grievances first reach the public and then later become part of the formal governmental agenda. Lipsky viewed such protest efforts on the part of powerless black groups as a sophisticated and conscious way of influencing public policy.[2] One central aim of political protest is to trigger the involvement of powerful groups who, in turn, seek to influence government officials in ways favorable to the goals of protest leaders. Among the prominent outcomes of this phase of the civil rights movement were the Civil Rights Act of 1964, the Voting Rights Act of 1965, and the Open Housing Act of 1968.

As the black civil rights movement matured and entered the electoral politics arena, Hispanics and American Indians, in part because of the successes of blacks, were also organizing for political incorporation. In the 1960s and early 1970s, Mexican-American activist organizations were formed, and these organizations came to be known collectively as the Chicano movement.[3] Unlike the (black) civil rights movement, which was national in scope because of the geographical distribution of blacks, the Chicano movement was concentrated principally in the southwestern states of Texas, New Mexico, California, Colorado, and Arizona. Various organizations evolved, including Movimiento Estudiantil Chicano de Aztlan (MECHA) and the United Mexican Students (UMAs), which sought responsiveness to grievances in areas of police brutality, the treatment of Chicanos by law enforcement and judicial organizations, job discrimination, housing inequities, and inadequate health care.[4] For a period, political power also was sought through the creation of a third party, El Partido de La Raza Unida, initially in Texas.

A second Hispanic group, Puerto Ricans, have a very different history in the United States than do Hispanics of Mexican descent. Puerto Ricans are more recent arrivals and are found mostly in New York City and other eastern urban areas. Since Puerto Rico is a commonwealth protectorate of the United States and its citizens are U.S. citizens, many Puerto Rican immigrants have continued to be involved in the politics of their island.[5] Like the Chicano community, however, the Puerto Rican community was affected by successes of the black civil rights movement. Puerto Ricans, many of whom are black, questioned their conditions in the urban centers of the eastern seaboard, and various political organizations were formed.

A significant number of the third major Hispanic group, Cuban Americans, arrived in the United States after the 1960s and settled mainly in south Florida. Unlike the other Hispanic groups, Cuban Americans are generally characterized by a more conservative political orientation and fervent anti-Castro, anti-Communist positions. Indeed, for many years, this group was preoccupied with politics in Cuba, primarily the overthrow of Fidel Castro.[6] After the ill-fated Bay of Pigs invasion of Cuba in 1961 and a series of other events, Cubans in the United States recognized that they were permanent residents of the United States and sought citizenship. As U.S. citizens, Cubans have represented a significant electoral and political force in state and local elections, particularly in Florida.

The issue of mobilization among American Indians is much more complex than for other groups. Although one may speak in generic terms about American Indians, there are a number of dimensions along which political mobilization occurs. Nagel suggests that American Indian mobilization is three-tiered:

Indian mobilization is along *tribal* lines when it involves organization and action by members of one tribe in pursuit of tribal goals.... Mobilization is along *pan-tribal* lines when it involves organization and action by members of more than one tribe acting on the basis of tribal affiliation in pursuit of tribal or pan-tribal goals.... Mobilization is along *pan-Indian* lines when it involves organization and action by individual Indians on the basis of Indianness and in pursuit of pan-Indian goals.[7]

As with other racial minorities, the 1960s was a time for political mobilization among American Indians. Much of this activity was sparked by President Johnson's Great Society programs. As Nagel observes, "The War on Poverty programs of the 1960s injected massive resources into a nascent Native American movement."[8] Pan-Indian organizations began to appear during this period as well. In 1968 the American Indian Movement (AIM) was founded, led by Russell Means. Additionally, other organizations sought assistance for particular projects from governmental sources other than the Bureau of Indian Affairs.

POLITICAL REPRESENTATION

In the late 1960s, minority movements entered a new era—marked by demands to achieve representation and full participation in national, state, and local political arenas, which also meant minority movements were involved in a second stage of the policy formulation process. The emphasis shifted from breaking down barriers to civil rights to exercising the newly bestowed right to vote. The elections of Carl Stokes as mayor of Cleveland, Ohio, and Richard Hatcher as mayor of Gary, Indiana, in 1967 represented the first major thrust of blacks for political power in large urban centers.[9] Since the late 1960s, there has been a rapid increase in the number of black mayors, council, and other elected officials. In 1987, the Joint Center for Political Studies reported that there were 6,681 black elected officials at the state and local levels.[10] And by 1987, of the six largest cities in the United States, four had black mayors—Los Angeles, Philadelphia, Chicago, and Detroit. And major southern cities such as Atlanta, Birmingham, and New Orleans also had black mayors. Similar strides were taken by Hispanics with the election of Henry Cisneros in San Antonio, Federico Peña in Denver, and Maurice Ferrer in Miami. By the 1970s in New York, Puerto Ricans had elected a U.S. congressman, a state senator, and several other state and municipal officials.[11] There is evidence, as well, that minority representation in elected office may result in more responsive municipal policies.[12]

Despite these essential electoral gains, it became apparent that minority elected officials alone were not sufficient. In addition, minorities would have to be well represented in key administrative positions, as well. Many important matters simply fall under the purview of public administrators. The lines between policy formulation and implementation are clear only in textbooks. Administrators are crucial to minority interests because of their myriad influences in formulating policy, in guiding and persuading elected officials in the development of policy, in interpreting the intent of policy, and in implementing—or failing to implement—policy. To secure fair treatment, to help assure favorable policy development and implementation, and to progress economically, minorities lobbied for the principle of representative bureaucracy, that is, government employment of minorities in proportion to minority representation in the population.

Numerous factors are important in the successful implementation of any policy. Sabatier and Mazmanian and Van Meter and Van Horn concluded that clarity of policy goals and objectives, in particular, are essential to successful implementation.[13] Among other conditions are a specific office responsible for implementing the policy, a staff favorable to the policy, and superiors supportive of implementation efforts. The absence of any of these critical conditions often signals the likelihood of implementation failure. Success of policies beneficial to minority citizens

INTRODUCTION: MINORITY ADMINISTRATORS

often is advanced when minority individuals are present in the implementing agencies. In view of the importance of the implementation process, it is clear that minority activism will not end with the election of minorities to political office, but must move into a third stage—full representation in administrative positions, particularly in this era in which political power has increasingly passed from elected officials to career bureaucrats.

Some would contend that various public administrators actually have more influence than elected officials over the policy arenas that directly affect the lives of minority groups. For example, if one is concerned about the relationship between the police department and minority communities, the appointment of a minority police chief may yield faster and more permanent structural changes than the election of a minority city council person or even mayor. Moreover, increases in minority employment may come more quickly if a minority person is hired as director of personnel, city manager, or agency head. One study found that the attitude of the director of personnel toward affirmative action exerted an influence on female employment success that was independent of community and organizational characteristics.[14] A similar situation may be the case for minority employment success, as well.[15]

Clearly, minorities in *elective* office are important in promoting systematic changes in the way that the policy concerns of minorities are addressed. Indeed, the appointment of minority administrators to key posts is only made possible through changes in the political environment—and minority appointments often follow the election of minorities to city councils and mayorships.[16] However, in the implementation of policy objectives, the presence of minority administrators is of great value. Holden has observed, "because implementation depends on specific administrative choices, those groups successful in penetrating the administrative process are likely to achieve a good deal of what they want, and those unsuccessful in penetrating the administrative process are likely to achieve relatively little of what they want."[17]

AFFIRMATIVE ACTION AND REPRESENTATIVE BUREAUCRACY

The principal vehicle through which representative bureaucracy is sought is through affirmative action, a set of specific and result-oriented procedures that are utilized to help insure that minorities and women are not disadvantaged in efforts to secure employment, e.g., recruitment, selection, retention, and promotion.[18] Stemming from authority in Title VII of the Civil Rights Act of 1964 and the Equal Opportunity Act of 1972, the Equal Employment Opportunity Commission has utilized affirmative action plans, both voluntary and compulsory, to increase the number of minority group members in state and local government.[19] Despite numerous court challenges, the basic principles of affirmative action have been upheld by the Supreme Court.

Advocates of representative bureaucracy contend that as minority administrators are brought into the administrative arena, these individuals will represent the interests of their respective communities, attempt to make government more responsive to minority policy concerns, and make governmental policies more understandable to their communities. The assumption of representative bureaucracy is that minority administrators will become advocates for their groups' interests, thereby allowing more access to the policy process and promoting policies which are more responsive to minority communities.

If one uses numbers of minority administrative officials as a surrogate for access to the policy process, one would have to conclude that access is limited. For example, the number of minorities in municipal administrative and appointive public service positions is extremely small. Table 1.1 shows the distribution of minorities in selected categories of municipal positions. Blacks are approximately 12 percent of the population, Hispanics are nearly 7 percent, and Indians constitute less than 1 percent. However, in 1987, of the 4,744 city managers in the United States, only 1.1 percent were black, 0.2 percent Native American and 1.6 percent Hispanic. Of the 1,272 assistant city managers, 3.7 percent, 0.4 percent, and 2.6 percent were black, Native American, and Hispanic, respectively. In the area of law enforcement, minorities do not seem to be faring much better. Of the 6,443 police chiefs in the country, 1.5 percent were black, 0.4 percent were Native American, and 1.6 percent were Hispanic.

CONSTRAINTS

As mentioned previously, the concept of representative bureaucracy assumes that minority administrators will represent the policy concerns of their communities. The assumption is that minority administrators will become advocates for their communities. Henderson, in examining the concept of advocacy among black urban administrators, defined advocacy in the following manner:

> When black administrators actively pursue the interests of black urban communities in the urban policy process, they are . . . engaging in advocacy. They transcend purely technical or professional conceptions of their roles. . . . The concept of advocacy therefore defines behaviors which are distinguishable from sharing a racial or social identity with a political or administrative constituency. These behaviors include specific actions taken by an advocate to pursue or to implement policy preferences articulated by persons or groups on whose behalf the advocate acts.[20]

INTRODUCTION: MINORITY ADMINISTRATORS

Table 1.1
Selected Minority Municipal Officials for U.S. Cities with Population over 2,500, 1987

	Total	Black	Native American	Hispanic
Chief Appointed Administrative Officer	4,744	52 (1.1%)	12 (0.2%)	80 (1.6%)
Assistant Manager/ Assistant CAO	1,272	47 (3.7%)	6 (2.0%)	33 (2.6%)
Personnel Director	3,088	108 (3.5%)	6 (1.0%)	67 (2.1%)
Chief Financial Officer	5,336	57 (1.1%)	10 (0.2%)	59 (1.1%)
Director of Public Works	5,716	99 (1.7%)	17 (0.2%)	98 (1.7%)
Police Chief	6,443	100 (1.5%)	27 (0.4%)	105 (1.6%)
Fire Chief	6,141	52 (0.8%)	13 (0.2%)	58 (0.9%)

Source: The 1987 Municipal Yearbook (Washington, DC: International City Managers Association, 1987), p. 287.

But is this assumption of representative bureaucracy correct? Clearly, minority administrators have no blank check. They can not simply undertake programs or initiate new practices simply because of their preferences. They are limited by a host of formal rules. Moreover, as Norton Long and others have suggested, role constraints are of great importance, as well, in patterning administrative behavior. When examining the behavior of minority administrators, particularly within the framework of the assumptions of representative bureaucracy, one needs to assess whether and how much formal roles and position rules constrain behavior. Thus a black city manager may be very committed to the needs and concerns of the black community, but the position may establish parameters on what action the manager is able to take. Holden addressed whether or not minority administrators automatically represent the interest of their communities:

> No executive appointee, no senior bureaucrat, automatically represents the "interest" with which he has, in the past, been most identified merely because of the past identification. The bureaucratic enterprise contains its own incentive which impose directions and constraints on the functionary. Thus, it is fatuous to expect that a black functionary will automatically "represent black interests" or that, if he attempts to do this he will be automatically effective, without some external relationships.[21]

Herbert discussed six forces which confront minority administrators, and which significantly influence their effectiveness and perceptions of their responsibility to their agency and minorities in general.[22] These factors are system demands, traditional role expectations, colleague pressure, community accountability, personal commitment to community, and personal ambition.

The first force, *system demands,* refers to the expectations of public employees that a governmental system reinforces through a system of rewards and punishments. Systems have ways of ensuring that individuals comply with the goals and objectives of the organizations and ways of sanctioning individuals who do not comply. For minority administrators, whom Herbert views as being the very best because of the intense scrutiny that minority applicants experience in the hiring process, the demand to comply without question may become an impediment to addressing the needs of their communities.

The second force is *tradititonal role expectations.* Herbert argues that minority administrators generally have been relegated to positions which almost exclusively deal with minority group issues. He believes that minority administrators need to spread throughout agencies in a variety of positions in order to have an impact on the policy process. This phenomenon is still a pressing issue, though there are some minority administrators, as indicated by the data in table 1.1, who hold positions with policy-making authority.

Colleague pressure is a third danger in impeding governmental responsiveness to the concerns of minority communities. The force is manifest in a variety of ways. For example, a minority police officer who wants to be accepted by his peers may be harder on minority offenders to gain acceptance or promotion. Or a minority supervisor may go out of the way not to hire minority group members to show no bias against whites or no favoritism toward minorities. Given the difficulty in fighting this type of pressure, minority administrators must put this peer pressure into perspective so not to overshadow program objectives and community needs.

INTRODUCTION: MINORITY ADMINISTRATORS

Over the last several decades, demands have been made for greater community control of policies and hiring minority administrators who would listen to the needs of minority communities. This has led to the assumption that minorities want and need administrators who understand the concerns of the community and are willing to listen and communicate with them. Thus *community accountability* is another force which impacts minority administrators.

Personal commitment to community is the fifth force, which Herbert sees as critical to addressing the needs of minority communities. The degree to which a minority administrator feels a commitment to the minority community will dictate the extent to which he will attempt to play a role critical to decision making relative to the needs and concerns of the minority community. If this commitment is lacking, then the desire to play the latter role will also be absent.

The final force is *personal ambition*. As the public sector has opened up employment opportunities to minority group members, the opportunities for advancement have also expanded. Given the fact that a limited number of minorities will be promoted to high-level positions, the problem for minority administrators is how to balance one's personal ambitions while simultaneously expressing a commitment to increasing government's responsiveness to the policy concerns of minority communities.

These forces, singularly and in combination, lead to several dilemmas for minority administrators. Among these dilemmas are:

- Governmental role expectations of minority administrators do not necessarily coincide with the minority administrators' own perceptions, goals, or expectations
- Unresponsive public policies put minority administrators in extremely tenuous positions vis-à-vis the agency, himself/herself, and the community of which he/she is a part
- Advancement within the governmental system is generally a function of adherence to established organizational norms; one of these norms historically has been that one need not be concerned about the needs and priorities of minority communities
- Minority communities sometimes expect much more of the minority administrator than he/she can provide; and in most cases demand a far faster response to their demands than these administrators have developed a capacity to deliver.[23]

Most minority administrators will find themselves confronted with one or more of these dilemmas during the course of a career. And, unfortunately, the nature of being a minority administrator, in a governmental system which has not always been responsive to the needs and concerns of minority communities, dictates that the administrator will experience pressures and conflicts that majority administrators will not experience. Moreover, their "racial loyalty" will be frequently questioned and used as a litmus test on many issues by both the minority and majority communities. Often, they will be placed in a "damned if you do, damned if you don't" situation.

PURPOSE AND OVERVIEW OF THIS VOLUME

Holden's and Herbert's views of the position of minority administrators provide a framework for analyzing the role of minority administrators and their impact on policy issues in urban politics. How closely does the theory fit the experiences of urban minority administrators? How much does the position constrain the role they play vis-à-vis minority communities?

This volume is the result of a conference, "Minority Administrators: Perspectives and Problems," sponsored by the School of Public Affairs at Arizona State University in 1986. The purpose of the conference was to explore some of the issues raised in the literature about the role of and importance to the policy concerns of minority communities of minority administrators. Moreover, we were interested in exploring the perspective minority administrators had of their positions and the problems, if any, minority group status had on their ability to do their jobs or advantages it afforded them. Additionally, we wanted to explore the dilemmas that the literature indicates minority administrators face.

An attempt was made to select urban minority administrators in high-level positions with substantial policy-making and decision-making authority. Also, we attempted, where possible, to have more than one minority group represented in these positions. Therefore, we invited a black and Hispanic city manager, a black and Hispanic chief of police, a Hispanic female political administrator, and a Native American female head of an urban quasi-governmental organization.

We formulated a set of questions to address some of the issues discussed above. Questions asked about were:

- Philosophy of administration and administrative style
- Innovations and new ways of management
- Major successes and apparent failures
- Preparation for current responsibilities
- Lessons from experiences that could be useful to other minority administrators
- Strengths and weaknesses as an administrator
- Policy-making discretion
- Major sources of support
- Relationship to minority communities and minority employees
- Goals with respect to the minority community
- Unique problems and opportunities encountered due to minority status.

Lenneal J. Henderson of the University of Tennessee is the author of Chapter 2. He discusses the notion of role elasticity of minority urban administrators. Rule definitions and responsibilities of minority administrators are explored.

Grace Montañez Davis, the deputy mayor of the city of Los Angeles, contributes Chapter 3. She describes the unique role that she plays and her relationships with the mayor; the city council; the city bureaucracy; and the black, Hispanic, and Asian communities of Los Angeles.

Sylvester Murray, the former city manager of San Diego, in Chapter 4 discusses his career path to city management. He also discusses some of the problems one encounters in being a minority city manager in a conservative city, the tough decisions that have to be made and relations with the city council and minority communities.

Chapter 5, by JoAnn Kauffman, the executive director of the Seattle Indian Health Board, discusses the particular problems of being a Native American administrator in a city where Native Americans are an "invisible," needy minority. She also explores the importance of networking with other minorities and the political lobbying role she has assumed on behalf of her organization and Native American peoples.

Joel Valdez, city manager of Tucson, is the author of Chapter 6. Valdez discusses the process of changing the complexion of the city bureaucracy and the problems encountered.

Chapter 7, by Reuben M. Greenberg, the chief of police of Charleston, South Carolina, discusses administration by a black police chief in the "birthplace" of the Old Confederacy. His unique administrative style, the reaction of police officers to that style, and his commitment to affirmative action are among the many issues treated.

Ruben B. Ortega, chief of police of Phoenix, is the author of Chapter 8. He explores the complexities of being a Hispanic police chief and the tensions that are created by the role. Also discussed are his management style and his commitment to affirmative action.

Chapter 9, by the editors, presents a concluding view of the role of minority administrators in urban politics.

Since this book blends the theoretical with the practical and explores salient issues of concern to minorities and public administration, we hope that this book will begin to fill a void in knowledge about minority administrators and their roles.

NOTES

1. Roger W. Cobb, Jennie-Keith Ross, and Marc Howard Ross, "Agenda Building as a Comparative Process," *American Political Science Review* 70 (March 1976):128.

2. Michael Lipsky, *Protest in City Politics* (Chicago: Rand McNally, 1970), p. 172.

3. Leobardo Estrada, Chris F. Garcia, Reynaldo F. Marcias, and Lionel Maldonado, "Chicanos in the United States: A History of Exploitation and Resistance," *Daedalus* 110 (Spring 1981):103–32.

4. Chris F. Garcia and Rudolph O. de la Garza, *The Chicano Political Experience* (North Scituate, Mass.: Duxbury Press, 1977), chapter 4.

5. Joan Moore and Henry Pachon, *Hispanics in the United States* (Englewood Cliffs, N.J.: Prentice-Hall, 1985), p. 186.

6. Ibid., p. 191.

7. Joane Nagel, "The Political Mobilization of Native Americans," *The Social Science Journal* 19 (July 1982):38.

8. Ibid., p. 42.

9. For a more detailed discussion see William E. Nelson and Philip J. Meranto, *Electing Black Mayors* (Columbus: Ohio State University Press, 1977).

10. Joint Center for Political Studies, *Black Elected Officials: A National Roster* (Washington, D.C.: Joint Center for Political Studies, 1987).

11. Moore and Pachon, *Hispanics in the United States*, p. 190.

12. For example, see D. Campbell and J. Feagin, "Black Politics in the South," *Journal of Politics* 37 (February 1975):129–159; William J. Keech, *The Impact of Negro Voting* (Chicago: Rand McKally, 1968); M. Jones, "Black Officeholders in Local Governments of the South," *Politics* 2 (March 1973):49–72; L. Cole, "Electing Blacks to Municipal Office," *Urban Affairs Quarterly*, 10 September 1974: 17–39. Albert K. Karnig, "Black Representation on City Councils," *Urban Affairs Quarterly* 12 (December 1976):223–42; Susan Welch and Albert K. Karnig, "The Impact of Black Elected Officials on Urban Expenditures and Intergovernmental Revenues," in D. R. Marshall, ed., *Urban Policy Making* (Beverly Hills, Calif.: Sage, 1979); Rufus P. Browning, Dale Rogers Marshall, and David H. Tabb, *Protetst Is Not Enough* (Berkeley: University of California Press, 1984).

13. P. Sabatier and D. Mazmanian, "The Implementation of Public Policy: A Framework of Analysis," *Policy Studies Journal* 8 (special issue no. 2 1980):445–88; D. S. Van Meter and C. E. Van Horn, "The Policy Implementation Process: A Conceptual Framework," *Administration and Society* 6 (February 1975):538–60.

14. Grace H. Saltzstein, "Female Mayors and Women in Municipal Jobs," *American Journal of Political Science* 30 (February 1986):140–64.

15. P. K. Eisinger, *The Politics of Displacement: Racial and Ethnic Transistion in Three Cities* (New York: Academic Press, 1980).

16. For more discussion see Welch and Karnig, "The Impact of Black Elected Officials on Urban Expenditures and Intergovernmental Revenues"; P. K. Eisinger, "Black Employment in Municipal Jobs: The Impact of Black Political Power," *American Political Science Review* 76 (June 1982):380–92; T. R. Dye and James Resnick, "Political Power and City Jobs: Determinants of Minority Employment," *Social Science Quarterly* 62 (September 1981):475–86.

17. Matthew Holden, Jr., *The Politics of the Black "Nation"* (San Francisco: Chandler Publishing Co., 1973), p. 204.

18. Michael W. Combs and John Gruhl, *Affirmative Action* (Jefferson, N.C.: McFarland & Co., 1986), p. 1.

19. Harrell R. Rodgers, "Fair Employment Laws for Minorities: An Evaluation of Federal Implementation," in Charles S. Bullock III and Charles M. Lamb,

eds., *Implementation of Civil Rights Policy* (Monterey, Calif.: Brooks/Cole Publishing Co., 1984), p. 97.

20. Lenneal J. Henderson, "Black Administrators and the Politics of Administrative Advocacy," in L. S. Yearwood, ed., *Black Organizations: Issues on Survival Techniques* (Lanham, Md.: University Press of America, 1980), pp. 54–55.

21. Holden, *The Politics of the Black "Nation,"* p. 206.

22. A. W. Herbert, "The Minority Administrator: Problems, Prospects and Challenges," *Public Administration Review*, vol. 34, no. 6 (November/December 1974):560–62.

23. Ibid., p. 562.

2

Urban Administrators: The Politics of Role Elasticity

Lenneal J. Henderson

INTRODUCTION

Public administration is as vital to the politics of race as any variable in the metropolis. Historically, good, just, and equitable policies, a recurring object of black and Hispanic politicians and activists, represented but a Pyrrhic victory without *implementation*, the actualization of public policy.[1] Morality in policy formulation and adoption failed to guarantee delivery of goods and services to nonwhites as a policy impact.[2] Consequently, black and Hispanic elected officials increasingly emphasize efficient, effective, and equitable administration in cities, counties, and metropolitan areas. However, as Horton recently observed, "while service delivery is but one of government's functions, its management has become an increasingly important concern; slower growth in public money places a high social premium on 'making the most' of government resources; public choice theory challenges the core assumption of many academicians that public management can become more 'competitive'; privatization, a policy derivative of public choice ideas, threatens the jobs of some practitioners," particularly public administrators.[3] Only the skill, knowledge, and ethics of the public administrator can maximize implementation in an environment of resource scarcity and organizational uncertainty.

Therefore, this chapter hypothesizes that urban public administrators, particularly black and Hispanic urban administrators, are essential variables in the politics of urban policy implementation, particularly in black and Hispanic communities. Their presence and ascendancy is largely the result of decades of civil rights advocacy and progressive public policy.[4] However, economic fluctuations, tax expenditure reform and limitations, deficit politics, and a general public opinion blacklash against affirmative action policies complicate the presence of black and Hispanic urban managers.[5] Not only must these managers deftly transcend the "normal" vagaries of urban management, they must manage the political, professional, interpersonal, and personal peculiarities of race and ethnicity.[6] The consequence is a multidimensionality in administrative roles quite unique in urban management.

Role elasticity is the concept developed in this chapter to analyze challenges faced by black and Hispanic urban administrators. How much role or many formal and informal subroles can these managers accommodate? How elastic are the roles? How elastic are role incumbents before a breakdown or collapse of role occurs? What are the sources of role strain, particularly when role expectations are largely inelastic, that is, incapable of accommodating advocacy or other dimensions desired by black and Hispanic administrative role incumbents? How possible is it for black and Hispanic administrators to avoid aspects of role expectations thrust upon them by the media? By superordinate elected officials? By the public-at-large? By black and Hispanic organizations or communities?

THEORETICAL PERSPECTIVE

Role elasticity is diversity, and often incompatibility, in the aspects of administrative roles. Formal role expectations are written in official job descriptions. Usually baseline in character, these job descriptions exclude informal role dimensions such as mentoring subordinate employees, public service, and professional activities. Urban administrators are expected to fulfill formal job requirements, serve as experts and counselors to mayors, urban legislators, and other politicians; exhibit responsiveness to a variety of urban citizen groups; maintain professional skills and knowledge and resolve any emergency arising in their domains.[7] Reconciliation of these diverse dimensions of role expectations must be ethical and professional.[8]

ROLE DETERMINANTS FACING BLACK AND HISPANIC PUBLIC ADMINISTRATORS

Adam W. Herbert has identified six key forces which confront minority administrators[9] and which influence significantly their potential effectiveness and perception of responsibility to governmental agencies and

URBAN ADMINISTRATORS

minorities in general (see figure 2.1).[10] These forces or determinants include:

1. *System Demands.* System demands are those expectations of public employees that a governmental system reinforces through a range of sanctions and rewards.

2. *"Traditional" Role Expectations.* The U.S. Commission on Civil Rights has dichotomized these expectations into "old traditional jobs" and "new traditional jobs." The commission argues that: "In addition to the 'old traditional jobs for Black Americans (mostly white-collar jobs in health and welfare agencies), new traditional jobs appear to be emerging.' These are usually jobs as staff members of human relations councils, civil rights commissions, or assistants to ranking administrators. They are status jobs carrying major responsibilities, and usually bring excellent salaries. But they remain almost exclusively related to minority group problems."[11] These jobs bring a civil rights orientation into urban administration and are part of what Burton Levy refers to as "the racial bureaucracy." Black and Hispanic representation in the traditionally crucial positions of finance, planning, public works, public utilities, and public safety remain minimal.[12]

3. *Colleague Pressures.* These are pressures from the peers of black and Hispanic administrators to conform to bureaucratic, professional, or, more frequently, informal personal norms and mores in the agency. These norms and mores not only tend overtly and covertly to discourage these administrators who openly advocate black or Hispanic interests, but they also compel minority administrators to practice or reinforce existing racist behavior in bureaucracy. These behaviors range from publicly blaming minority agency clients for their own socioeconomic misfortune to firing nonwhite employees who become outspoken for other nonwhites.

4. *Community Accountability.* The civil rights, black power, and community control movements of the 1960s stressed greater neighborhood involvement in urban political and administrative decision making. Bolstered by the citizen participation requirements included in antipoverty, model cities, and housing programs funded by the federal government, ghetto residents clamored not only for more accountability from public administrators but also for more hiring of minority public officials who presumably would be accountable and more responsive to their needs. The apparent lull in social and community action in the mid–1970s has not lessened this demand. The demand is clear. Minority people want and need administrators who will listen to them, who can communicate with them, and who care about them.[13]

5. *Personal Commitment to Community.* Akin to the demands by neighborhoods for more responsive administrators, particularly in the 1970s, is the need for a personal commitment of minority administrators to the community. The degree to which the administrator feels that there are obligations to fulfill and a role to be played which only they can fulfill can make a critical difference in public policy discussions, decisions, and, ultimately, service output.[14]

6. *Personal Ambition.* A seldom stated but critical variable among black and His-

Figure 2.1
Role Demands on Minority Administrators

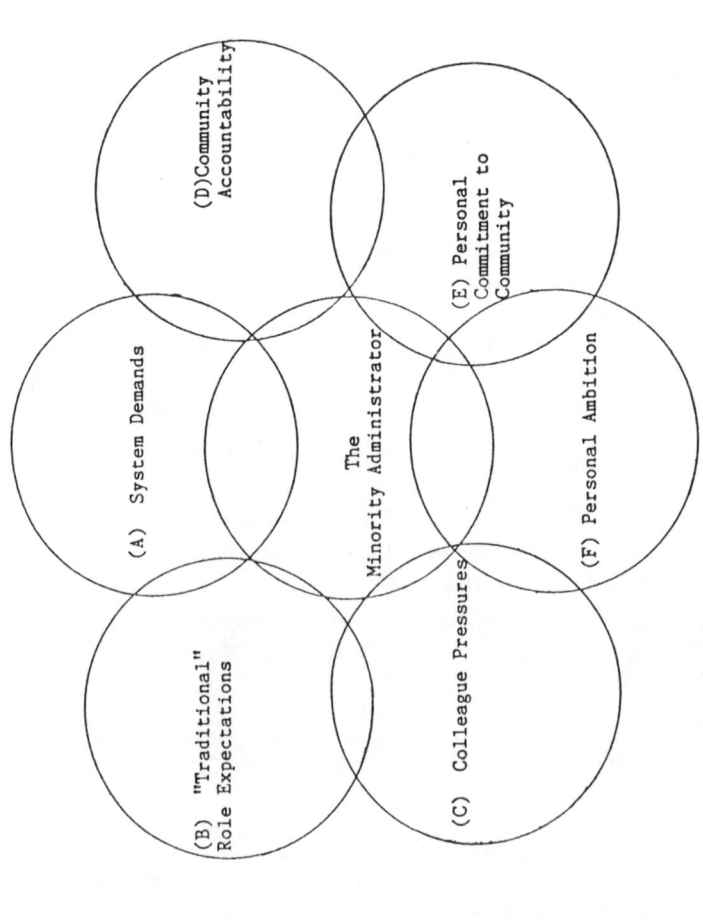

(A) System Demands

(B) "Traditional" Role Expectations

(C) Colleague Pressures

(D) Community Accountability

(E) Personal Commitment to Community

(F) Personal Ambition

The Minority Administrator

Source: Adam W. Herbert, "The Minority Administrator: Problems, Prospects and Challenges," Public Administration Review, n. 34, v. 6, November/December 1974, p. 560.

panic administrators is their own personal ambitions in the career or political world. The way in which these administrators respond to the conflicting pressures of administrative superiors and community activists is apparently calculated to insure returns to their own aspirations. The reward/deprivation system manifested in bureaucracy's control of the minority administrator's paycheck, legitimacy, authority, and reputation usually plays a greater role in determining their choices than the more moral/political imperatives of community leaders in black and Hispanic communities. Moreover, equal employment opportunity and affirmative action requirements in the Civil Rights Act of 1964 and the Equal Employment Opportunity Act of 1972 mandated that urban administrative agencies recruit more black, as well as other nonwhite, administrators. This encouraged administrative nomadism among black administrators, the propensity to use the opportunities affirmative action policy affords to flee one job for another when either job pressures are too great to endure and/or job opportunities elsewhere are too attractive to resist.

Personal ambitions of black and Hispanic administrators become more important as their educational attainment increases. These factors may combine to preclude occupational complacency in these administrators. Some black and Hispanic administrators interviewed in the study conducted by Henderson openly admitted that they keep one eye on their present jobs and one on emerging job opportunities elsewhere.[15] What may encourage this ambition even more is the relative paucity of minority administrators in public management and the consequent incessant search for them by personnel officers seeking to satisfy affirmative action requirements. Age, education, and job experience coupled with opportunity and demand may fuel the personal ambitions of minority administrators.[16]

These six role determinants identified by Herbert specify both the components of the minority administrator's role environment and the minority administrator's personal disposition toward that environment. Although white urban administrators confront the same role determinants, various civic and community and professional organizations—some black, some white—are salient forces in the minority administrator's environment. These forces are frequently external to the minority administrator's agency and role. But a second and more immediate component of the minority administrator's role environment is the urban bureaucracy. Systems demands, colleague relationships, and organizational hierarchy within administrative agencies are included in the web of interpersonal, professional, and bureaucratic relationships which comprise the administrator's role and function.

Administrative roles are more than mere job descriptions. Administrators pursue their own interpretations of job descriptions as they pursue and negotiate official roles. Herbert's inventory of role determinants may provide the active context for minority administrators but the minority administrators ultimately decide what weights to assign to the various role demands. How minority administrators relate community/

civic, professional, and bureaucratic elements to their own personal aspirations and commitments may suggest both the relative importance of community and agency reference groups in their value frameworks as administrators, and more particularly, how minority administrators define their agency roles.

But, in the context of this chapter, administrator advocacy is defined as the actions pursued by urban administrators on behalf of a group, policy, plan, or fiscal choice. Contrasted with traditional definitions of "representative bureaucracy," administrator advocacy pursues interests, not just passive representation of racial, regional, gender, or other specific demographic groups.[17] Advocacy can be built into administrative mandates or occur as informal and discretionary administrative action. Figure 2.2 describes the various configurations of advocacy models as developed by Henderson. Three points interrelate these advocacy models to Herbert's six role determinants of minority administrators: First, systems demands, colleague pressures, and "traditional job expectations" correspond to issues associated with internal and intermediate advocacy models. Second, demands for community accountability and a personal commitment to community correspond generally to external advocacy models. Third, the intersection and articulation of the professional, bureaucratic, and advocacy dimensions of the minority administrator's role essentially reflect the balance of importance these administrators assign to each dimension. Thus, personal ambition becomes the expression of the minority administrator's educational, civic, and occupational socialization; their concessions or capitulations to agency superiors and colleagues and their own personal needs. Personal ambition therefore converts these role determinants into the administrative behavior associated with black administrators.

Moreover, these six role determinants suggest not only the context in which urban administrative roles operate but also the opportunities and constraints minority urban administrators with advocacy propensities are likely to encounter. While the nature of these constraints vary from agency to agency and city to city, they profoundly affect minority urban administrator advocacy.

THE CONCEPT OF ADMINISTRATIVE ADVOCACY

Herbert's role determinants illustrate the problem of role elasticity, the continuous stretching and intermingling of official and informal role dimensions. Advocacy is a facet of role elasticity. Advocacy is the active, deliberate, and consistent pursuit of a defined interest. Administrative advocacy is the active, deliberate, and consistent pursuit of a defined interest by a public organization or agency. In a sense, all public agencies are advocacy organizations by definition. They ostensibly pursue the public interest.

Figure 2.2
Advocacy Models

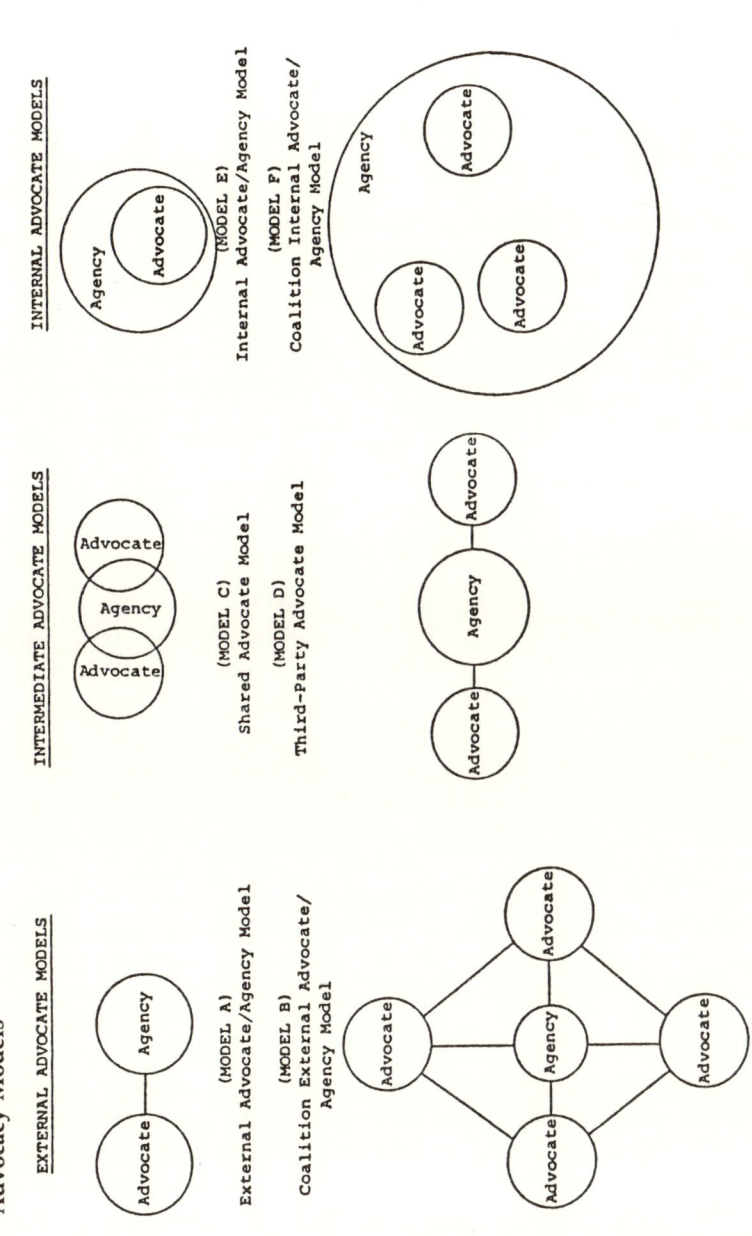

EXTERNAL ADVOCATE MODELS

(MODEL A)
External Advocate/Agency Model

(MODEL B)
Coalition External Advocate/
Agency Model

INTERMEDIATE ADVOCATE MODELS

(MODEL C)
Shared Advocate Model

(MODEL D)
Third-Party Advocate Model

INTERNAL ADVOCATE MODELS

(MODEL E)
Internal Advocate/Agency Model

(MODEL F)
Coalition Internal Advocate/
Agency Model

Source: Lenneal J. Henderson, Administrative Advocacy (R & E Research Associates, Inc., 1979), p. 17

Whether the minority administrators are mere racial "representatives" in a bureaucracy or continuous advocates of what their communities define as their interests depends upon their response to bureaucratic, professional, or community role demands. Any administrator who fulfills agency role expectations is more likely to acquiesce in racial/symbolic representation and to eschew advocacy. Those black and Hispanic administrators more concerned about fulfilling the expectations of their communities by making a personal commitment to pursue *actively* the interests of those groups move beyond mere symbolic representation to advocacy. However, dichotomization of urban minority administrator commitments to agency and community may be spurious if the agency's mission defines an advocacy role for these administrators. Affirmative action officers, human relations commissioners, social workers, community health administrators, and others find an advocacy dimension built into their official role definitions. These built-in advocacy dimensions make minority urban administrator's commitments to agency and client expectations coincide rather than conflict. But, regardless of built-in advocacy dimensions in minority administrator roles, it is possible that the urban minority administrator may wish to go beyond official agency advocacy to become more politically active in the client community.

Of course, it is also possible that these administrators may not go as far as advocacy dimensions of official agency roles require. The dilemma of the black and Hispanic administrator in either instance is that, although black and Hispanic clients through community organizations may demand that these administrators be more *accountable* to them through personal commitments, the minority administrator's *authorization* to act derives from urban bureaucracies. How these administrators resolve this dilemma determines not only whether or not they become advocates for black and Hispanic interests but also whether they choose internal or external advocacy strategies, that is, whether they advance community interests by using their administrative role to confer with superiors or whether they join and participate in community organizations outside the agency, or both.

Finally, the intensity of black and Hispanic administrator advocacy will consist not only of the presence or absence of advocacy dimensions in the minority administrator's official role definition but also of the strategies and consistency with which minority administrators advocate black and Hispanic interests. The resort of internal, intermediate, and external forms of advocacy all cumulate into an intensity continuum for administrator advocacy.

But the relationships between role and advocacy concepts: (1) express the political as well as the technical/administrative position of minority administrators; (2) reveal the position of these administrators in a web of conflicting role expectations, particularly when community and agency interests are irreconcilable; (3) suggest the adaptive capacity of urban bureaucracies confronted with rising demands from black and Hispanic communities to adequately accommodate those demands through administrator advocacy; (4) facilitate discussion of the framework and process by which minority administrators sort out and negotiate their roles, particularly when they seem torn between community and bureaucratic demands; and (5) provide insight into the intensity and strategies black and Hispanic administrators with advocacy tendencies pursue.

However, to develop an adequate portrait of minority administrator advocacy, three additional variables seem critical. First, some description of the socioeconomic characteristics of the population of cities, counties, or multijurisdictional agencies employing black and Hispanic administrators provides an overview of the larger context in which both these administrators and their respective agencies operate. The demography, racial composition, per capita income, educational level, employment, spatial distribution, housing, and other attributes of these populations constitute the general, social, economic, and political environments in which urban agencies operate. Within this general socioeconomic enivronment, however, is the specific service or target population with which black and Hispanic administrators interact. This population provides the immediate context for minority administrator advocacy. Whether the service population is predominantly black or white, rich or poor, highly organized or without organization, or very dependent or minimally dependent on public services are critical context variables that may or may not engender a personal commitment by black and Hispanic administrators to use formal administrative authority to alleviate community problems.

RELATIONSHIP OF CIVIC, COMMUNITY, AND PROFESSIONAL ORGANIZATIONS TO MINORITY ADMINISTRATORS

Particularly important is the level of community interest group organization in city or neighborhood areas with grave socioeconomic problems. Most of these areas have received massive injections of federal and local housing, social services, and other assistance through the actions of their community organizations. How black and Hispanic administrators interact with these organizations, particularly those serving as advocates for clients of urban bureaucracies the minority administrator works in is important as an instance of union between external (community) advocacy and internal (black/Hispanic administrator) advocacy.

Moreover, a variety of neighborhood and citywide organizations seek to provide special services to minority urban populations. The Urban League Opportunities Industrialization Center, Operation PUSH, League of United Latin American Citizens (LULAC), and a variety of other national and local organizations not only continuously demand equity and responsiveness, recognition and services from urban government but also provide employment, training, housing assistance, information and referral, health and other services to blacks and Hispanics through governmental subsidy.

The "Great Society" programs of the 1960s—the Manpower Development and Training Act (MDTA), Model Cities, the Economic Opportunity Act, and others—enhanced community advocacy through citizen participation requirements and federally subsidized neighborhood programs. Demands for community control and affirmative action in private and public hiring practices increased as minority neighborhoods became more politically active. When blacks and Hispanics were recruited as public officials, minority neighborhoods expected them to be particularly sensitive to their needs and aspirations.[18]

Despite the apparent lull in the intensity of community militancy and the switch from categorical grant-in-aid "Great Society" programs to revenue-sharing approaches in the 1970s, the demands of minority urban populations for bureaucratic responsiveness through minority public officials has not diminished. Cities, counties, special districts, and other jurisdictions conducting programs in black and Hispanic communities have hired more administrators in these communities. Minority administrators abound in equal employment, employment training, community development, and social services programs serving predominantly their own populations. Since the administrator's immediate clientele in these programs is nonwhite, they not only are importuned to speak for neighborhood interests but confront the ire of neighborhood residents if they fail to do so.

Conversely, urban minority administrators working in public agencies with predominantly white employees and/or serving predominantly white clientele may assume a different posture than those serving predominantly nonwhite populations. Frequently, these agencies are not characterized by an explicit racial orientation in their program. They may be fiscal, public works, computer, or other agencies without a social service mission.

Thus, the socioeconomic environment of urban agencies, the nature of the clients they serve, and the level of community or political organization of those clients seem critical variables in the study of minority administrator advocacy. The programs of urban agencies and the advocacy of community organizations both purport to grapple with and resolve the myriad problems suggested by socioeconomic data in urban areas. To know what the nature of those problems are establishes an appropriate framework for assessing any activity designed to change this environment.

A second additional variable germane to minority administrator advocacy is the structural/functional character of urban governments and agencies that they work for and that ostensibly serve urban populations. The organizations, fiscal capacity, personnel classification, and bureaucratic style of city, county, and metropolitan-wide agencies are, along with the socioeconomic characteristics of the service population, major determinates of administrative behavior. As indicated earlier, urban governments are the most immediate environments minority administrators must accommodate. These environments either impose constraints on or provide opportunities for constructive forms of advocacy.

The relationship of the nonwhite administrator to both the urban government and the nonwhite urban population ultimately depends upon the size, mission, and policies of the urban agency. But several characteristics of urban government seem particularly pertinent to the minority administrator's position in the agency and their relationship with nonwhite urban populations: (1) the visibility of the agency or government in the black and Hispanic communities, that is, how well the agency is known by community leaders and organizations; (2) the formal organization of government into mayor-council, council-manager, commission, or other forms. These forms suggest the relationship between the policy-making and administrative process and the availability of public hearings, advisory process, and other opportunities for black and Hispanic input; (3) continuing with number 2, the presence or absence of citizen participatory institutions in government; and (4) the nature of the agency, department, or administrative subdivision the black or Hispanic administrator is responsible for, i.e., whether they head the public works department, the controller's office, or the affirmative action division seems to determine the appropriateness of advocacy for nonwhite interests.

Finally, the role of professional organizations in the black and Hispanic administrator's conception of role must be identified and related to other role determinants. Professional organizations are sources of occupational legitimacy, peer group exchange, job-related information, and most importantly, standards of professional behavior against which job roles may be evaluated. In his study of police professionalism, Maniha has developed the following model of professionalization:

1. Development of specific theory or intellectual technique
2. Relevance to basic social values
3. A training period

4. Motivation toward an ideal service
5. Autonomy
6. Sense of commitment
7. Sense of colleagueship or community
8. A code of ethics.[19]

Professional organizations are agents of professionalization continuously establishing and updating the elements in Maniha's model. Professional values and norms articulated and defended by the International City Management Association (ICMA), the American Society for Public Administration (ASPA), the International Personnel Management Association (IPMA), and other administrator-oriented associations may impact upon minority administrative behavior and, thereby, minority administrator advocacy. Professional standards and codes of ethics often include references to appropriate advocacy activities for those in the administrative profession.

It is important, however, to be precise about the black and Hispanic administrator's adherence to the norms and standards of professional associations and groups. It is important to establish that these administrators actually join and participate in these professional organizations and that their behavior is actually influenced by professional standards and values. It would seem that black and Hispanic administrators seeking to establish "professional legitimacy," particularly among white peers, would join established professional associations. Often, however, these associations may not overtly encourage advocacy for minority group interests alone. As Adam Herbert argues:

to the minority administrator goes the challenge of accepting the obligation of working for the development and operation of public programs which more effectively meet the needs of all people. In some cases this may require an advocacy position. It may demand that the minority group perspective on public policy questions be researched, developed and articulated. It will frequently demand the capacity and willingness to discuss policy options, directions, and needs with those who have expressed a lack of faith in the governmental process. It will demand a rejection of the argument that administrators are/must be value-free and completely neutral in implementing policy decisions.[20]

One emerging development which seems to combine professionalization with the semblance of commitment to black and Hispanic communities is the proliferation of minority employee and professional caucuses. These organizations usually emerge from the predominantly white, "mainstream" professional associations representing administrators, personnel specialists, fiscal experts, planners, and other executive public servants. They are frequently motivated by both dissatisfaction with the attitudes and lack of commitment of predominantly white associations to black and Hispanic members and black and Hispanic clients and a perceived need for more focused attention to the needs of minority professionals and the larger minority community.

Examples of these new professional organizations include the Conference of Minority Public Administrators (COMPA), the National Association of Planners (NAP), the National Association of Black Social Workers (NABSW), the National Association of Black Psychologists, and the National Association of Black Lawyers. Although inchoate, stronger in some metropolitan areas than others, and frequently fluctuating in membership, financial support, and activity, these organizations constitute a kind of professional and administrative enclave and refuge from the racism of their predominantly white counterparts.[21] Often, these associations sponsor programs for the recruitment and training of more black and Hispanic professionals and for community-based technical assistance programs. These programs are also intended to combat what they perceive as racism by whites and the maldistribution of goods and services to ghetto areas. For example, the Conference of Minority Public Administrators, the National Forum of Black Public Administrators, and the National Association of Hispanic Elected Officials have conducted workshops for minority administrators in federal, state, and local governments; academicians; students; and other interested persons.[22] The International City Management Association has also operated a Talent Data Bank Program linking minority persons with executive, administrative, or policy-making job opportunities. Moreover, both the National Association of Black Social Workers and the National Association of Health Services Executives have considerable impact upon their members' perceptions of the role of the minority professional in health and welfare organizations. But these associations may represent only a segment of the nonwhite professionals and administrators within their respective occupations. Indeed, their resources seem meager and their organizational infrastructure seems more developed in the southern, western, and eastern United States than in other regions. This regional imbalance in membership strength and resource allocation may reflect the larger, more well-entrenched black and Hispanic populations in these regions of the nation; and the presence of black colleges and universities able to promote black associations, particularly throughout the South.

Ultimately, how effective these professional associations are as advocacy instruments depends upon their leadership, goals and objectives, resources and strategies. Some associations are national; others are regional or local. Some depend upon a small core of leaders for most of their dynamism and program; others are more structurally and functionally differentiated and hierarchical as organizations. Some associations are racially or ideologically more militant than others. Some are subdivisions, committees, or affiliates of predominantly white professional associations; others are organizationally independent of white professional groups.

Strategically, some minority professional associations seek to bolster and to unify the number and activities of blacks and Hispanics in their respective professions while others concentrate on racial reform in predominantly white organizations. Some of these professional organizations are active in ghettos and barrios while others seek policy reform at the national, state, or local levels. Some organizations pursue several or a combination of the above-mentioned strategies.[23]

Thus, added to Herbert's six role determinants are three additional role considerations: (1) the socioeconomic environment of urban bureaucracies which employ black and Hispanic administrators; (2) the structure and function of urban governments employing these administrators; and (3) black and Hispanic administrator membership in white and/or minority-focused professional associations which may influence their advocacy perceptions, attitudes, and behavior. When these three elements are added to systems demands, colleague pressures, "traditional" job expectations, community accountability, personal commitment to the community, and personal ambition, it is obvious that the categories relate and overlap considerably. But how the minority administrator sorts and assigns priorities to them in his own administrative behavior and converts them into advocacy activity ultimately varies with both the urban agency and the administrator.

THE CHANGING CONTEXT OF URBAN ADMINISTRATIVE ADVOCACY

The foregoing discussion of administrative advocacy underscores the dilemmas of role elasticity facing black and Hispanic urban administrators. Excessive role stretching results in often unbearable strain for these administrative incumbents. Coping strategies range from drug addiction and alcoholism to frequent job changes and negative interpersonal behavior. Six challenges face minority urban administrators in the 1990s:

1. Deciphering and accommodating urban socioeconomic needs in the changing demography of cities, particularly metropolitan areas with substantial black, Hispanic, immigrant, indigent, and other needy populations. According to the Population Reference Bureau, 76 percent of the U.S. population lives in the nation's 281 metropolitan areas.[24] During the 1980–86 period, U.S. metropolitan areas grew by 4.5 percent, as compared to 3.4 percent for the national population outside of the metropolis.[25] In the West and Southwest, Hispanic and Asian populations grew almost twice as fast as white populations, and in the South, East, and Midwest, black populations grew signifi-

cantly faster than white populations. Both rapidly increasing black and Hispanic populations reflected increasing need for public support and improved social services delivery. Minority administrators will be a key element in accommodating those increased needs.

2. Reconciling personal, professional, technical, civic, and advocacy dimensions of urban administrative roles—the problem of *role elasticity*.
3. Alignment with the politics of policy directions of urban elected officials to whom the minority urban administrators are accountable.
4. Public relations management: the handling of media coverage and characterization—politics of novelty.
5. Management of resource constraints.
6. Establishment and maintenance of productive interpersonal and intergroup relationships inside the metropolitan bureaucracy and across that spectrum of the urban community most essential to the administrator's role and jurisdiction.

These six challenges configure themselves in a variety of shapes and sizes depending upon the demographic, socioeconomic, political, and economic context of the city, county, or metropolitan area.

OPTIONS AVAILABLE TO MINORITY URBAN ADMINISTRATORS

Given the difficulties of role elasticity, the challenges of administrative advocacy, and the demographic and socioeconomic challenges in the environment of urban management, urban minority administrators should consider:

1. *Use of administrative discretion.* This term describes the latitude or freedom that administrators have to act on their own in the absence or the ambiguity of statutory mandate or administrative rule or regulation.[26] Discretion may be used for advocacy, particularly when the spirit of the agency mission is promoted.
2. *Continued use of professional associations.* Both majority and minority professional associations are essentially resources for urban minority administrators. In addition to publications, conferences, training institutes, and other services, professional associations provide networks for engaging in what Holden refers to as "the politics of collective psychiatry."[27]
3. *Education and training.* Urban minority administrators with substantial experience and expertise in accommodating the problems of role elasticity should work closely with both majority and minority institutions of higher education and facilities like the International City Management Association to train both majority and minority public managers in successfully addressing role elasticity problems.
4. *Alignment and agendas of urban minority administrators with urban minority elected officials.* It is particularly important for urban minority elected officials to be

assured that policy priorities are effectively, efficiently, and expeditiously implemented. The key to effective implementation lies not only in program delivery, adequate fiscal resources, and support from the urban political leadership, but also from flexible, adaptive, and technically skilled urban administrators. Consequently, it is essential that the urban minority public administrator reconcile advocacy, technical, personal, and political agendas not only for him/herself and urban politicians to whom they are accountable, but also, for the sake of urban dwellers both majority and minority, whose accelerating needs require such support.

NOTES

The author wishes to express his endless and profound thanks to Dr. Paula McClain of Arizona State University, Georgia Persons of Howard University, and Cathy Benson of the University of Tennessee at Knoxville for their generous assistance in the preparation of this manuscript.

1. On the theory of implementation, see Jeffrey Pressman and Aaron Wildavsky, *Implementation* (Berkeley: University of California Press, 1973); Carl Van Horn, *Policy Implementation in the Federal System* (Lexington, Mass.: D. C. Heath, 1979), and Eugene Bardach, *The Implementation Game* (Cambridge: MIT Press, 1977).

2. On the concepts of "policy formulation" and "policy impact," see Thomas Dye, *Understanding Public Policy*, 45th ed. (Englewood Cliffs, N.J.: Prentice-Hall, 1986).

3. Raymond D. Horton, "Expenditures, Services, and Public Management," *Public Administration Review*, vol. 47, no. 5 (1987):378.

4. See Lawrence C. Howard, Lenneal J. Henderson, and Deryl Hunt, eds., *Public Administration and Public Policy: A Minority Perspective* (Pittsburgh, Pa.: Public Policy Press, 1977).

5. Lenneal J. Henderson, "Beyond Equity: The Future of Minorities in Urban Management," *Public Management*, vol. 64, no. 6 (June 1982): 2–3.

6. Lawrence C. Howard and Deryl Hunt, "Black Administrators in Urban Bureaucracy," *The Journal of Afro-American Issues*, vol. 3, no. 2 (Spring 1975).

7. Role theory contributes significantly to the analysis of administrative behavior. See, for example, Neal Gross, Ward Mason, and Alexander McEachern, *Exploration in Role Analysis* (New York: John Wiley and Sons, Inc., 1958).

8. On the relationship between professionalism and administrative responsiveness, see Richard C. Kearney and Chandan Sinha, "Professionalism and Bureaucratic Responsiveness: Conflict or Compatibility," *Public Administration Review*, vol. 48, no. 1 (January/February 1988):571.

9. The term "minority" includes American citizens with African, Spanish-speaking, Asian, Pacific Islanders, or Native American ancestry.

10. Adam W. Herbert, "The Minority Administrator: Problems, Prospects and Challenges," *Public Administration Review*, vol. 34, no. 6 (November/December 1974):556–63.

11. U.S. Commission on Civil Rights, *For All the People, By All the People* (Washington, D.C.: U.S. Government Printing Office, 1969), p. 118.

12. See, for example, Lenneal J. Henderson, "Public Technology and the Metropolitan Ghetto," *The Black Scholar* (March 1974):9–17.

13. Herbert, op. cit., p. 561.

14. See Laurence E. Lynn, Jr., *Managing Public Policy* (Glenview, Ill.: Scott, Foresman Company, 1987).

15. Lenneal J. Henderson, *Administrative Advocacy: Black Administrators in Urban Bureaucracies* (Palo Alto, Calif.: R & E Research Associates, Inc., 1979).

16. Lenneal J. Henderson, "Administrative Advocacy and Black Urban Administrators," *The Annals* (September 1978):68–79.

17. Examples of the "representative bureaucracy" literature include Kenneth John Meier, "Representative Bureaucracy: An Empirical Analysis," *The American Political Science Review*, vol. 69, no. 2 (June 1975); and Samuel Kroslov, *Representative Bureaucracy* (Englewood Cliffs, N.J.: Prentice-Hall, 1974).

18. Henderson, *Administrative Advocacy*, op. cit., p. 26.

19. John K. Maniha, "Structural Supports for the Development of Professionalism Among Police Administrators," *Pacific Sociological Review*, vol. 16, no. 3 (1973):317.

20. Herbert, op. cit., p. 563.

21. Richard Monteih, "Placement in Action," *Public Management*, vol. 57, no. 11 (November 1975):3.

22. See Rose Robinson, "The Conference of Minority Public Administrators," *Public Administration Review*, vol. 34, no. 6 (November/December 1974):552.

23. Charles L. Sanders, *Black Professionals' Perceptions of Institutional Racism in Health and Welfare Organizations* (Fairlawn, N.J.: R. E. Burdick, Inc., 1973).

24. A Metropolitan Statistical Area (MSA) is a county or group of counties that contain either a city of 50,000 or more or an urbanized area of 50,000 or more and a total population of 100,000 or more. A Consolidate Metropolitan Area (CMA) is a large urban area that contains one million or more population.

25. "Metro U.S.A. Data Sheet," *Population Today*, vol. 15, no. 12 (December 1987):4.

26. Mark W. Huddleston, *The Public Administration Workbook* (New York: Longman, 1987), p. 187.

27. Matthew Holden, *The Politics of the Black "Nation"* (San Francisco: Chandler Publishing Co., 1973).

3

Los Angeles: Racial Diversity, Change, and Administrative Coordination

Grace Montañez Davis

INTRODUCTION

First, I would like to give you some background on the city of Los Angeles to give you an idea of the environment in which I work. Los Angeles is the second-largest city in the United States, with a population of about three million people. The 1980 census indicated that the city was 28 percent Hispanic, but it is probably more than that because of the large influx recently of Central American refugees. Twenty-four percent of the population is black, and added to that are the Ethiopian and Haitian refugees that somehow do not get counted yet. The Asian community in 1980 was listed as about 6 percent, but we have had a large influx of Korean, Filipino, and other Asian groups who add to that population. The only population that is fairly constant is the Native American, and they reside principally in the county and the surrounding parts of the city. In the Los Angeles School District, for instance, we have eighty-seven languages that are spoken, so when we speak of bilingual education, we are not just speaking about Hispanic children.

Tom Bradley, the first black mayor, was elected in 1973 after serving as a councilman for two terms. Of the fifteen council persons, three are women, three are black, one is Asian, and one is Hispanic, which is interesting since Hispanics are the largest minority population. The Hispanic council member is the first Hispanic in about twenty-eight years—Councilman Roybal who later became a congressman was the first Hispanic council person in the modern period of the city. An Asian and a Hispanic were both elected last year.

There are thirty-five departments and bureaus, and about 22,000 city employees, of which about 8,000 are in the police department. The city budget is well over $1 billion, which is not as large as it sounds when you see that the school district's budget—separate from the city—is over $2 billion.

PROBLEM AREAS

One of the principal areas of concern is housing. There is less than a 2 percent vacancy rate in the city, which accounts for overcrowding in many of our poorer neighborhoods. Often, especially in refugee communities, it is not uncommon to find two, three, and four families living together. Some of them work at night and others in the daytime. The ones that work at night take care of the kids during the day, and then they reverse roles in taking care of children. Because of limitations in funding and the lack of available space in the city, last year we completed only about 6,000 housing units.

Unemployment is another major problem. We pretty much stay at the national unemployment average, which right now is about 7.4 percent. But it is as high as 11 percent in some of the districts, and in minority communities, especially among young people, unemployment can go as high as 45 percent.

Paradoxically, we have some of the finest schools, but we also are troubled with overcrowding. For building-utilization purposes, we now have year-round schools. There are 35 to 45 percent dropout rates in schools that are predominantly minority. Currently, 50 percent of kindergarten students are Hispanic but, unfortunately, many Hispanic and other minority children do not get beyond the eighth grade.

Transportation is also a major problem. We have been struggling to obtain Metrorail funds from the federal government, and as you know, the Reagan administration has really been cutting back on the amount of money available in this area. They have made commitments, we have made plans based on those commitments, and, of course, we have had to cut back because we are not going to get the kinds of funds promised. We also were cut back on the People Mover, which was intended to move people through the central part of the city.

Another area related to transportation is traffic. Everybody in California drives. When we go to the corner store, we drive. And so there is great congestion on the streets. We have formed a new transportation department to help alleviate some of the congestion. Interestingly enough, they have been able to address it and solve congestion at sports events. For the area around the Colosseum, we have a sophisticated computer system, located in the city hall with a computer and a screen, and controllers can tell exactly the way traffic is moving and they can push buttons and get the traffic regulated. We have lots of freeways and, again, we are trying to alleviate congestion there. We have lanes, for example, used by those who participate in programs where people commute to and from work together. We also have similar lanes for buses.

Toxic waste is an emerging issue. You would think that only in the highly industrialized areas would you have that kind of problem, but we have the problem of getting rid of the waste of the manufacturers in the many industrial areas of our community. Many companies were dumping in empty lots near schools, near homes, and our children are having different kinds of allergies as a result of being exposed to fumes and paints. Dumps are another problem we have in relationship to toxic waste. Communities have finally discovered that dumps eventually start emitting gas and other odors with time. So communities are rebelling against the establishment of dumps in urban areas. We are now looking to burning rubbish, going way back to when we had incinerators, but this time it will be done electrically and controlled by the city.

Planning is also a major issue. We have twenty-eight communities within the city of Los Angeles. Many communities have their own identity and their own chamber of commerce, although they are part of the city. We have community advisory committees established in every community, and we actually hold public hearings on every aspect of proposed plans so people can come to the meetings and express either their aversion to or concurrence with various provisions. This procedure is used for commercial buildings, as well. Right now there are four councilmen who are trying to get an issue on the ballot that will limit the establishment of small shopping centers and establish height restrictions for commercial buildings. In the central city, we have buildings that are up to seventy-five floors high, but they want to limit this kind of growth in smaller communities.

RESPONSIBILITIES

My own formal responsibilities have changed over the years. Orginially, when I was director of human resources, I established the Office of Youth Services; the Agency on Aging, a volunteer office; an office for the handicapped; and an advisory committee for child care. The Office of Youth Services is still in the mayor's office. The agency on aging has become a separate city department. The volunteer program is very minimal except within some of the departments, because we lost funds from the federal government. The Office of the Handicapped is probably one of the largest programs and is still in the mayor's office. The city is going to try to establish child care facilities for employees within city hall and also for the city employees who work downtown at the Civic Center.

Grants

As a deputy mayor, one of my main responsibilities is to secure grants. At one time, before Reagan, our grants were as big as the city budget. We had over $900 million worth of federal and state grants that came to the city for everything from training and employment to housing and community development, aging, police, crime prevention, youth, voc-rehab, and the handicapped. We have had considerable cutbacks, as other cities have experienced. However, my main responsibility is to preserve processes as established by city ordinance in which all applications have to come through the mayor. We transmit them to the city clerk and to the grants council committee. There are three council members who sit on that committee and I sit for the mayor, although I do not have a vote. Once they are reviewed by that committee, the applications go to the council for their review and their vote. They then come back to the mayor for legal review and his signature. He is signatory to all contracts between the city and any other government agency. I do not personally do the reviews but I have staff and city attorneys work with me on reviews. The biggest problem I have had there is to preserve the mayor's political authority within the whole system, because councilmen would like to assume total authority. We want to maintain a checks and balances system on who gets the grants and make sure we are in compliance with federal regulations. It is advisable that the mayor's office remain an integral part of that system. In addition, we make sure that minorities bid on contracts and that they have equal access to contracts.

Budget

Let me explain the budget process. We have a chief administrative office that is an extension to the mayor's staff. Then we have a chief legislative analyst office that is an extension to the city council's office. The two offices always generate and review budgets, and make a presentation to the mayor prior to our sitting down with each general manager to negotiate the cuts or the items that they want reinstated. There really is no money now. Some of the managers will argue, e.g., the police and fire departments, recreation and parks, and maybe general services, and the city attorney. The city attorney, by the way, and the comptroller are both elected officials, so they feel that they can come in and argue, but the mayor is still in control of the budget. We leave council members alone. They just know that they only have so much funding and can spend it any way they wish, so it is difficult to regulate.

The budget process starts in October. There is an analyst from the CAO's office assigned to each department. Analysts work with officers to develop department budgets. By the end of February or the early part of March, we sit down and it takes us two weeks of review with the managers. The budget has to be to the city council by April 20. Council members go through the whole process all over again. They just have to show that they are also on top of things, and they have their finance committee review and then they have public deliberations. As you are aware, the budget undergoes changes during this process. The mayor has the ability to veto any changes that the council makes to his budget. He will justify why he vetoes changes, though sometimes he will allow certain alterations. An example of that is last year there were council members who insisted that we could add a thousand new police officers to the police department, but the mayor felt that the money needed to go elsewhere and that the police department could look for other ways of cutting administration costs and putting police out on the street. We won that issue when it went to the ballot.

Interdepartment Coordination

Each department has a commission made up of private citizens appointed by the mayor. We try to balance representation on the commissions as to geographic area of the city, gender, and professions that can add to the functions of the department—members who can review contracting and budgets and so on. We also strive for minority balance on each commission. The general manager handles the day-to-day operations of each department. I get involved in overseeing all of these departments. I obviously do not get involved with the day-to-day operations, but there are many times when there is a policy issue in which a department is trying to accomplish something and needs to know whether the mayor will approve and give support as the policy goes through council and other obstacles may have to be overcome. Departments generally will come to me, and if I know the mayor's position on such issues, I will express it to them. If not, then I will take it to the mayor or ask the general manager to go see the mayor personally.

There are many things we do that require coordination of one department with another. A department does not tell another what to do, and so a representative will come to me and say, "We're gonna be involved in this particular thing." I will bring them all together and we will decide what in particular applies to any department, and who is going to be responsible for certain things. We all then know and I keep tabs on whether or not the job gets done, and they all have to report back to me. I also deal with departments when a council person or a constituent complains. To give you an example, I had a baker whose power had been turned off and he was accusing the Department of Water and Power. I talked to the general manager, he assigned staff to it, and we looked into it. It turned out the man had twelve years of bad business with the Water and Power, but at least I was able to assure him that he had gotten a fair review of the situation.

Constituents

My other major responsibility has to do with constituents. The city is broken into five geographic areas and we have one staff person assigned to each. They, in essence, are the ears and eyes of the mayor out in the community. They attend community meetings to listen and to see if there is a role for the city. If citizens are putting on a fund raiser, maybe they want to borrow some chairs from the city, or a stage, sound equipment, and so on—a staff person is there to facilitate that kind of a request to the city. They also, of course, attend social functions or installation banquets and so on and present commendations on behalf of the mayor and the city. Those five people are also responsible for all of the correspondence that comes to the mayor. The mail is broken down by zip code and as it comes into our document center, it is distributed according to zip code to each of those persons. They also are responsible for all the phone calls that come in. If somebody calls, we will ask them, "What is your zip code?" and we will transfer the call according to the zip code. All of the letters that are written for the mayor's signature come to me and I look at them for continuity and consistency on an issue. If there is an issue on which we are getting a lot of letters, we will develop a form letter response so that everybody is using the same answer. I also look to see what are the issues, what are people concerned about.

There are four major areas right now in which I have full responsibility. One area is concerned with refugees, either from South America, Ethiopia, or Haiti, and we have a representative advisory committee that I chair. The second area is the homeless. I head up a task force for the city and county which decides not only where we get money for housing but where we get money for mental health problems and regular health problems. Again it is a coordinating effort. I have to bring all kinds of people together for that. AIDS is the third area for which I have responsibility. Nobody else wants to touch it. The gay and lesbian community is a fourth area of responsibility that I respond to. The men do not like to go to the gay-issues meetings, but it does not bother me; so I go.

Since I am a woman and a minority, I have my own constituency. Women in the city identify with me and want me to come to their meetings. They want me to be a part of this and a part of that, and I try to be as responsive as I can, not just in the city but anywhere up and down the state and in fact in the United States. The same is true with minorities, because before we had an Hispanic elected official the people looked to me and I played that role, although I was not elected. I attend many, many functions that have to do with minority communities—not just Hispanic but also Asians and blacks. In fact, I worked in Watts for a long time when I was there with the Department of Labor, and many people just thought I was black; I say I am a black who speaks Spanish and I get away with it.

One other function that I perform for the mayor has to do with press conferences. After he finishes a press conference, I will then do the same press conference in Spanish for the Spanish language news—we have several television stations and quite a few newspapers and radio stations. Thus, I usually have to be prepared to be responsive on all of the issues.

International and National

I get involved on the national and international level, too, which I enjoy tremendously. We have an office of protocol and we get to meet people like Prince Charles, heads of state, artists, and leaders in minority communities around the world. When Bishop Tutu was in Los Angeles, I was very honored to meet him. There have been many dignitaries during the years, and, of course, we get to attend many of the functions related to their visits.

I was privileged to represent the city on the Social Security Council during Carter's administration. That was a national council and I commuted to Washington once a month during a two-year appointment. We made many recommendations, which are continued in a book, and that's probably as far as they will get. Under Carter's administration, I was also a member of a national advisory committee to the commissioner of immigration, and that was very interesting. We travelled all over the country and did a border patrol tour and a lot of things that let you see the problems first hand.

I currently sit on the State Advisory Committee to the National Commission on Civil Rights. And when Senator Julian Bond referred to Clarence Pendleton, I knew exactly what he was talking about. I knew Clarence from San Diego. I also sit on the Superintendent of States Advisory Council on Hispanic Affairs in the state of California. Once a year I go to Mexico on an official tour or trip with several organizations in Los Angeles arranged by the Office of Tourism. I am very pleased to have met both the current and previous presidents of Mexico. I met them when they were campaigning and subsequently in their formal capacity. In fact, I went to the installation of President Lopez Portillo of Mexico. I have been to Berlin representing the city, talking about planning, transportation, and housing. I am going back there in September to talk about their minority problems. They have problems with Turkish immigrants that they import for labor needs. I have also been on a mission—an Hispanic mission to Israel. Again, I was the only woman who attended and everything was done in Spanish.

Basically that is an overview of what my job entails. I am sure I have left out a thousand things because I work at least a twelve-hour day, and weekends, you know, maybe six hours on Saturday. I try to avoid Sundays but sometimes I cannot. But I really enjoy my work. I think it has been a great experience. I do not know what I am going to do when I am not deputy because I am spoiled, really.

PRIVATE LIFE

I do not have any private life. I am divorced. I cannot imagine what would happen if I were married. My children—let's see, ten years ago they would have been about twenty, eighteen, and sixteen—resented my job because I would tell them they had to behave so we would not embarrass the mayor. They would say, "Well, who is he? He's not our father." They really love him though and have never given us any problems. However, when they were younger I had to have a housekeeper who took care of them, especially when I travelled; but when I travel I always call home. When I am in the office I always tell the secretaries that if God or my kids call, interrupt me because I am a telephone mother and I have to be available to them. They so seldom call that you do want to be available to them.

What I have learned to do now that they are older is to schedule them in the calendar just like I do anyone else, and if it is going to be someone's birthday we put it on the calendar and I do not schedule anything else. There are times even now when I have vacation and I do not want to go anywhere because I travel so much; I just want to stay home and I will be there and I say, "Well, I'm home!" and they say, "Yeah, but we have to go over here," or "We have to go over there." I only have one at home now, my youngest son who is twenty-six. My oldest daughter, who repairs computers, doesn't have a college degree but she is doing very well. My second daughter is a geneticist and is a graduate of USC and Brown University and is now back in Los Angeles doing research. She clones whatever! My son is in his senior year at Cal Poly Pomona and is going to be an architect.

But as for personal relations, there is no way in the world for me to have one. There just is not a man in the world who wants to play second fiddle because even when I go to an event, I do not sit still. I hop around to the tables saying hello to people, because if you do not say hello to people they are going to remind you that you were there and you did not say hello. It is all votes for the mayor somewhere along the line. That is something that you can never get away from. You have to make sure you are not turning people off. You have to respond to phone calls.

I call people late at night if I happen to have their home number. They are always surprised, but then it is better to call at that hour than not to call them at all.

The other disadvantage is that a lot of times you cannot tell when people are trying to get near you or close to you because they want something. That happens so many times that you just learn not to get close to people after a while. So it does affect your private life.

Once, during an interview, I said I had no private life. The mayor had a press conference the next day, and he introduced me by saying, "She was complaining yesterday because she says she has no private life. Why should she have one? I don't have one." So I figured that was the last time I was going to complain.

ADMINISTRATIVE PHILOSOPHY

My philosophy of administration can best be typified as loosely structured "management by objectives" which has been developed over the years of my experience in government. In my various professional positions, I have had the opportunity to be both a manager and subordinate working with and under administrators with varying management styles and philosophies. I learned from each manager—both consciously and subconsciously—those styles which I felt best suited my personality and my sense of how a certain project should be managed or how a mission should be accomplished.

Although my formal training was not in public administration, I certainly have had ample opportunities over the years to work with and manage individuals that have had such training. While in the main I have found that such training is important, in the realm of human dimensions or people problems, the most important elements needed to be an effective manager are to be sensitive to suffering; be willing to listen and really to hear and understand the message that is being conveyed to you by citizens, constituents, or whomever; be able to respect individuals regardless of their position or station in life; and be forthright in attempting to find a resolution to the problem at hand. By all of this, I mean to say that there are human qualities and certainly common sense that must be exhibited by a manager or administrator whether or not they have a graduate degree in administration.

The resolution of conflict is and perhaps will always be one of the most difficult areas faced by any manager or administrator—whether we are talking about personality conflicts within the confines of an office, a strike by employees, disparate political groups, or racial tensions—this is the most taxing challenge to be faced by persons in positions of responsibility and one is never really adequately prepared initially. I have learned on the job and acquired the skills of an effective negotiator, mediator, and arbitrator who can bring people together and attempt to work out agreements and hopefully resolve a conflict or dispute so that the parties feel they have been dealt with equitably and can live with the agreement.

There are a great number of theories as to what is the best approach in motivating employees and constituents—certainly in my work we think of motivating constituents to support our administration—but whether we speak of employees or the body politic, we are talking about influencing human behavior in such a way as to meet the mission at hand. Motivation can best be developed when there is effective communication and an understanding of the job to be done. We have to talk about one's ability to lead, commitment to professionalism, and ability to set an example as a leader that will instill trust and a sense of commitment in one's subordinates. People can be motivated to participate in the accomplishment of a mission if they feel that they have a personal stake—be it compensation or an altruistic end.

Let me say just one thing about being an administrator in a political setting. It is different than if you have a straight administrative environment because you may be the best organized person and have plans to get the job done, but a press conference or something else may change your whole day. The unpredictable nature of the job probably has kept me from being frustrated. You have to learn to be flexible. For instance, I have been there for ten years as a deputy—and I have had three companion deputies over time. The other deputies were what I call the hardware, and I am the software, because they dealt with the issues but do not deal with people as I do. I know that Ray Remy, who was the national president of the Association of Public Administrators and was used to dealing more routinely, would pull his hair out every once in a while because he just had to set everything aside and proceed to address whatever the issue was that happened to come up. Also, you have political considerations to contend with. I refer to the fifteen council members as fifteen egos because every one of them is *the* king in his or her district. And you have to take them into consideration no matter what you do. You keep them informed. You give then courtesies in letting them know what you are doing in their district because otherwise, later on, when it comes to a vote, they may not vote with you.

I think one of the capabilities that I have developed as an administrator is knowledge. I am a very resourceful person. I am always being called from the outside, from within the city, and from our own staff and being asked if I know something about an issue or if I know somebody that can help them. The reason that is possible is because I am a generalist. I really feel an administrator should really be generalist. You cannot think that you are going to focus on just one aspect of whatever the function of your office is. It just does not happen that way. You will get problems and things that occur that are not within that realm. So you have to learn to know what is happening all around you.

When I meet somebody I will keep business cards—I have tons of business cards, and when somebody asks me about something, I will say, "Well, gee, you know, I met so and so." Or if I read something as things come across my desk, I will refer back to the business card file. Somehow I have managed to register all that kind of information and when people will ask me I will remember and I will pull a card from our files. Even as I am reading them, rather than keeping it myself because it is not something that I am really going to use, I will write somebody else's name on it and have it sent to them. And it does not have to be somebody in the office. It can be somebody in Arizona.

Some people are interested in issues. Other people are experts in issues. I try to put them together so that when people come to me, I seem to be able to say, "I don't have that information now but let me call you back." I make a few phone calls and get the information. I have a real knack for doing that and I think information and assistance are important things people look for in a minority administrator.

I am part of the most historic, exciting, and productive administration in the history of Los Angeles. Tom Bradley's success, and certainly mine, has been rooted in the fact that he brought persons into his administration who have understood his mission, philosophy, and vision for Los Angeles. The mayor established the parameters of his administration and they have been wide and flexible enough to allow staff creativity and ingenuity to bring about major public works projects, revitalization of communities, a renaissance of the arts, and unparalleled economic growth and development of our business community. I mentioned these things because not only have I had a great amount of discretion in developing policy, especially in the area of human rights, affirmative action, and the design and implementation of our grant-funded programs, but so have a majority of our administrators. They have succeeded because they were given a vote of confidence and trust by this administration and encouraged to put their best ideas and projects forward.

INNOVATIONS AND SUCCESSES

Let me deal with innovation and the new ways of management first. Back in 1980, everybody was talking about the decade of the Hispanics. At the same time we saw cutbacks in the sources of money for all program areas. So we decided to start looking through the Community Development Department at what our funding sources were, where our money was going and how we could do some creative leveraging of monies. For instance, we had $10 million of old Office of Economic

Security money that we were getting on an annual basis. Well, in Los Angeles that is not very much because of the great number of organizations that we have. But then we also had public service money from the Community Development Block Grant. So we devised this incredible formula. We sat down and we talked and strategized with the staff, and we came up with a plan that we presented to council in terms of putting funds together.

It was a *major* undertaking to convince the council that we should use this formula. But we were able to fund more organizations and at a higher level of funding by putting together the money. By the way, we continue to do that. For instance, this year with the Gramm-Rudman cutback we are still *not* going to have any cutbacks or closing down of agencies because we are shifting monies and putting it all together in one pool.

Another innovation is the development of a system of advisory committees and task forces. For instance, after we had Proposition 13 and lost access to property taxes, we brought in an advisory committee of financial people to review the city's finances. Now that is the first time we have brought outsiders in to look at the city. We got a lot of support from the private sector. They made certain recommendations that we were able to implement.

At one time, we have had as many as fifty-eight advisory committees counseling the city on one issue or another. They are not permanent, because they are there for a particular purpose, for a particular issue. Once we have a solution to a current problem, the committee may not serve anymore. But it is a good way to have participation in our government and to let people know that we have input from the people that are being affected. In fact, we always insist on what we call consumer representation on any committee or task force that we appoint.

In housing production, for instance, I brought together the three departments: the Community Development Department, the Community Redevelopment Department (which has all that tax increment money), and the Housing Authority. Before they were competing with one another to generate housing, but bringing them together permitted everyone to see what communities they were serving, the possibilities of exchanging land, and of leveraging some of the funds that they had. And so we were able to get higher housing production.

The close cooperation of these three departments has also been helpful in generating/issuing municipal bonds. For instance, last year the Community Development Department reached its limit. So the Housing Authority issued bonds to generate houses for community development. Currently, we are looking at a formal merger of those three departments. Since Housing and Urban Development is drying up the well, we are going to have difficulty having enough money to support three different administrations. Therefore, we are studying the merger of those three departments. The redevelopment agency is fighting a merger because it has the most money and it is tax money, not government money.

I mentioned one success and that was to have the mayor's authority survive within the grant system. Council members wanted to take that on their own and it was only by my perseverance—not being loud, not being overbearing in terms of the authority, but dealing with the city attorney, dealing with the wording of the ordinance, and getting the city attorney to give an opinion—that we were able to survive. I think it is being able to deal with people, understanding how not to be contrary with them.

The other successes that I think I have had, as I mentioned, are with the community: dealing with them, keeping them rather than alienating them, and making them feel that they are a part of the system.

I have been very successful in convincing council members from more affluent areas that certain federal money must go to poorer areas. I tell them when we have other pockets of money, where poverty is not the criterion, we certainly will give your district a fair hearing. But it takes a lot of talking and unruffling feathers and assurances to do that. It takes time.

My failures, I think, have been that I sometimes procrastinate too much. I tire sometimes of all the paperwork. When I am procrastinating, I go down the hall and visit with other staff members. So I am not really wasting my time because I am finding out what they are doing, how they are doing. But it gets me away from my office, it gets me away from my paperwork.

My management of time, as I said, is a problem because you may be well organized and attempt to do things but when you come in that is not what you do. So getting behind in my paperwork is one failure. Although I say that I never, never go home without emptying my "in" box, and I empty my "in" box at least three times a day, that is how much paper I get because I get everything that is generated by departments, and the paper is how I keep on top of what they are doing.

I cannot ignore my "in" box because all of the payments that are made through grants go through my office, and I sign off on them because I know the budgets. So I cannot hold up any payments. Every day, any time I walk in my office the first thing I do is to pull whatever is in my "in" box. There are papers to sign. I sign those right away, then move them on. Things that go to the mayor go on a special route sheet and again I sign off on those and just quickly glance at them. You develop a system but you get tired of paper after a while.

PREPARATION AND LESSONS LEARNED

If I was to single out any one area in my background out of the host of jobs, experiences, and circumstances that have contributed to my growth, I would have to look to my experience and life in the community. My youth and certainly adult years in the multiethnic and multicultural community of Lincoln Heights prepared me to deal with the responsibilities of having to work in a city as diverse as Los Angeles. Additionally, my later years at college and graduate work at UCLA and the years in government that followed each brought with them new and important experiences, but clearly my roots and the experiences of my most formative years—interacting and making friends with the people of my community—gave me the needed insight, sensitivity, and understanding of human relations that are critically needed by any person in a position of leadership in a city like Los Angeles.

I have never had a structured education in either public administration or business administration. I really bemoan that fact. When I went to work for Tom Bradley, I was going to go to law school, but my appointment was the end of that. I do try to get to as much of the training that is made available to our managers. I just enrolled in a master's program that is being given for managers. When I have gone to the university to speak to public administration classes, the professors refer to me as a practical administrator because I learned on the job.

I have learned by observing people. I observe successful people, people that I can work with, people that I have been able to work with, people who have been helpful, and people who are productive and generated ideas for the city. I get close to them because I want to see how they accomplish their objectives. I have had students in my office who were majoring in public administration and working for their doctorates or their master's. I could tell that they were making a contribution to me as a person and to the office, not just in the speeches they were writing but in the way they carried out assignments, the way they analyzed problems, and the way they presented them to me or to whomever. I learned, and I would ask them questions about the theories behind their work.

I think that all of us should always look to the world around us, particularly in administration, so that we can learn. For instance, I do not mind calling the personnel manager and telling him, "Look, I have this problem in personnel here. Will you either give me some background or can you tell me what would be the best way to handle it?" The personnel manager knows me very well and I think he probably appreciates the fact that rather than institute my own approach to solving problems I am trying to utilize an established method. I try to educate myself. I go to seminars and lectures. I also subscribe to an executive workshop series in which different issues are dealt with on a monthly basis. There are also many kinds of training sessions that I go to during lunchtime or on the weekends.

Let me just add some other points in terms of strength as an administrator. When a problem has been identified, I try to study the problem or the project thoroughly before making recommendations. I bring experts together to develop a consensus on problem solving when it is necessary. Also important is the ability to train effectively and motivate subordinates on whom I must rely and delegate responsibilities. I am a great delegator. Even as behind as I am with all the paper work, I still would be even more behind if I did not delegate. I have one administrative assistant who helps me and I have pretty much delegated entirely to her areas of AIDS and the homeless, because there is no way that I could respond to all the phone calls. It is very important to learn to delegate. Also I have the entire city to delegate to. If I need a speech; if I need a study to be done; or if I need a report to be read, reviewed, and analyzed; I send it out to the relevant departments.

My strengths are in developing trust with colleagues and community people in order to effectively mediate and negotiate agreements on various community issues and in organizing community and professional groups.

I think that in addition to the various areas of human relations and the need for sensitivity to people that I have outlined, which I think are vital, we then have to add to the formula the various academic ingredients and the disciplines that must be taken into account in developing a successful administrator. I certainly am an advocate of strong academic preparation in a professional or vocational field. Although my first direction in life was toward the life sciences and medical research rather than public administration or politics, I can, in retrospect, see areas where a more formal study of administration early in life would have been very beneficial. As deputy mayor, I have had the pleasure of working with a number of young people, some of whom I know to have considered me as their mentor, who during their tenure in my office were either working on their academic degrees or had just completed their degrees. We owe to our citizens the finest administrators possible to run increasingly complex governments.

Public administrators today must understand the complex budgets of cities, the increasing problems of insurance liability for city departments, the need of meeting rising expectations of citizens for services along with the demands for more cost effective municipal agencies, problems related to planning, zoning, fire and police services. Along with that today we must deal with the issues of human relations, affirmative action, and minority and women business enterprises. In Los Angeles and other major cities, we now must enter into areas such as international trade and commerce and the issue of immigration and sanctuary.

I mentioned the continuing tug-of-war between the various levels of government. Whether it be questions of jurisdictions with the county and the state government, or federal agencies over the appropriation of budget for rapid transit systems or diminishing federal aid in support of block grants, the public administrator of today must clearly be ready to meet a host of challenges. In a day's work those challenges may include everything from a constituent complaint about a barking dog to an international dispute over which flag to fly at city hall on a certain Chinese national day, because we have people from Taiwan and people from Mainland China.

The point is that we need talented, versatile, and eager professionals with well-planned academic training that, hopefully, has mitigated the parochial and myopic view of the world that often affects Americans. In a nutshell, you really need to be prepared. Because of my lack of training as an administrator, I have tried to be prepared for whatever the issue is, especially if I am going to be doing something with other departments. If I am not prepared, I get someone else to be the spokesman and all I do is chair the meeting; but the buck always comes back to me. I recently had a meeting with some developers who were complaining about how slow the city was in issuing permits and making inspections. I brought all the departments concerned together and they generated reports. However, I was the one who distributed them. I was briefed by each department on responses so that I was able to answer questions. You just never stop doing homework.

In addition to some of the areas that I have already covered, which I would apply in a general sense to both my subordinates, colleagues, and persons with whom I have to interact, I would include my ability to: study a problem or project thoroughly before making recommendations, to bring experts or knowledgeable people together to develop consensus, to effectively train and motivate subordinates on whom I must rely and delegate responsibilities, develop a relationship of trust with colleagues and community people in order to effectively mediate and negotiate agreements on various community issues and/or problems, and organize community and/or professional groups to deal with an issue, a problem or situation within the community or the city at large.

COMMUNITY RELATIONSHIPS

First of all, I think that my major sources of support within the majority community come from women's groups. They see me as a woman first and my color second. I get an incredible amount of support from women all over and I get invited to a lot of groups. I also get support from labor people because my political education came out of the labor movement. When I was going to graduate school, I got involved in a lot of community issues, and in those days almost any organization in the community had a labor committee. They generally provided the leadership for political activities, so I got to know the labor leaders and I know I can count on them. If I am involved in a political campaign, I can go to labor leaders in almost any of the areas—the important ones to me are the retail clerks that give food, the butchers who give lunch meat, and the building trades who will provide people power for toting people around in their cars. So those are two important support elements in the majority community.

Because I am Hispanic, I do have a constituency within my own minority community and in other minority communities as well. One of the reasons that I have this support is that I do not sit at my desk and pontificate about my past experience or anything else. I actually get out on the street and I attend meetings of organizations. For example, the board of one of our cultural centers was having some internal problems. I spoke with both sides; then I sat in on a meeting. They have developed a great deal of respect for me, first, because of my age and, second, because I have been a participant.

Minority communities expect me to attend social and political functions. I not only am invited to give speeches but also to participate as a member of the audience. I like to hear, to listen, to express my opinion as a person. As an example, when Richard Alatore was elected to the city council, he left a vacancy in the assembly for which there was an election. He supported his former administrative assistant for the position and got some of his friends in the legislature and the mayor to endorse the same person. Well, I live in that district and since that would be my representative, I told the mayor that I could not just sit back because I could not endorse that candidate. I did not ask him; I just told him. I said I was going to endorse Mike Hernandez, who is a local young man who has been involved in the community. Now, his comment to me was: "You're going to raise hell." And I said: "Well, I'm used to that." So just before I came over here, I went public and endorsed Mike Hernandez, so they are raising hell while I am here. But the community is used to seeing me involved in things like that. I think that is how you get a constituency.

I get a great deal of support from organizations in the Asian community. Many times you do not have to do anything for them specifically, but you must listen and try to give guidance and motivation. I have done a lot with the Asian community. With the gay community it is the same thing. If I ran for office tomorrow, I could count on the entire community. It has not been just a relationship where I approve of everything they do. I once had a screaming match with one of the gays. I called him a bitch and I told him: "What hat do you want me to put on? My Mexican hat, my woman hat, or what hat?" And I said, "You don't have a history like these other minorities of having to struggle. So you have to wait your turn; you have to work your way to that position." So I have a very up-front relationship.

My relationship with minority communities within the city and the employees within my organization is similar. We have ethnic employees' associations within the city for every minority group: an Asian employees' association, a black employees' association, and a Hispanic employees' association. We also have a woman's affirmative action association. All of these groups have representation on the Affirmative Action Task Force, of which I am coleader with a man. I make sure that I attend the installation dinners or go to one of their membership meetings, or speak, or go to receptions which we have for them in the City Hall Tower. I try to do at least one event with each. If they have a scholarship program or if they are raising money for scholarships, I try to show up at least to one event. I like to let them know that I am there, that I am participating with them. Our affirmative action meetings are at seven o'clock in the morning on Thursdays, and they know that I am there, that I am committed. I go to retreats that we have on affirmative action, so they know I am there. I do have a very good relationship with those organizations.

There have been times, for instance, when the community does not want me to endorse a candidate because it feels that because I am a public official, my endorsement carries a lot of weight. When Richard Alatorre was running for city council, I endorsed him publicly only because he had a lot of political experience as an elected official and was the kind of a person that we needed to fill the shoes of the Irishman that had been representing Hispanics for eighteen years. I thought that the weight of his experience would be equal to and maybe even greater than that of the Irishman. The other Hispanic candidates did not like my endorsement and demanded my resignation or my firing, but they never left a phone number where I could call them back.

I have a special relationship with the community in regard to funding. I feel it is important to educate them and tell them the procedures for securing funds and who are the leading people to contact if they want to participate. I will take the time or ask the staff to attend when we have public hearings or bidders' conferences. What has to be done is to make sure that all our people learn what the system is. So they may be mad at me because they did not get their money, but they usually go away happy because next time they will be able to do better. I do this with all the different communities.

We work very closely in Los Angeles with the Mexican-American Administrators Association and with Mexican-American educators. I always try to attend their annual conferences, but if they are involved with a particular kind of project, such as a drop-out project, I try to help them secure money or just serve as a visible part of the program. For instance, I sit on Honig's council. Another thing that is important is to tell administrators that when they have an issue that is important, e.g., promotions or bilingual education, they need to let the rest of us know because we are their constituents and we can support them in whatever it is that they are advocating. So we need to work together.

By the way, Larry Gonzales, the new Hispanic representative on the Board of Education, is excellent. He does not have a college education. I think he worked for the school district as a community relations person during the desegregation process, and he was only twenty-seven when he was elected. He has done a lot to change things. He has gotten the board to put the lottery allocation aside until legislation is passed to allow the money to be used for school construction. Plus he got the board to place a magnet school on the east side for medical services (he has been influential in placing magnet schools all over the city). He quit his job with Senator Art Torres and is devoting himself full time to the school board. I am sure it hurts financially, but he is dedicated.

I am very encouraged about the generation of young people that is coming forth. They have a better command of the language than my generation did, they are better educated because there have been more opportunities, and they are coming back and recognizing that they have to provide a service to the community. I go all over the country and cannot believe the talent that I see. For instance, there was a conference at UCLA, a seminar on Chicano history. There were historians, both professors and graduate students of history, who were studying the history of Chicanos. I did not know we had women who were majoring in Chicano history like that. They were not talking just history, they were talking about the theory: How to write a history, what are the elements, how you authenticate facts. I just sat there and marvelled.

This made me realize that we do have people, we just do not know about them. It is bubbling and someday it is going to hit the surface. These minorities will be recognized. So there is hope for the generations after me.

Minority employees many times will come to me about grievances, even though it is outside of the chain of command, because at some point they feel they are not getting equitable treatment. I will listen to them and I will go and talk to their supervisors. If there is still some portion of that chain of command to be completed, I will only listen and then tell them that I have to wait until they finish going through the system. There have been times when I work behind the scenes. There was one employee who wanted to transfer to another unit. Her job had been eliminated when we had some cutbacks and she wanted to transfer to Water and Power. Although they had nine openings, Water and

Power employees were not willing to give one up for this woman who was going to be out on the street. It was up to the Civil Service Commission to make that determination. So I lobbied the commissioners in the background by phone and then I showed up and had coffee with them before the meeting. I never said a word. I was just there to show them that I was going to view their deliberations. They decided in favor of the woman. Since the woman was going to end up on the street and the other employees were only looking for promotions, I thought my action was justified. There are times, however, when it does not matter what you tell grievants. They will not accept your recommendation. On the other hand, there are people who have sent me flowers because I listened to them.

We have a Hispanic-Jewish dialogue and a black-Jewish dialogue, and the blacks and Jews really went at it publicly recently. What got blacks angry was that they and other minorities perceive that the mayor was more responsive to the Jewish community than other minority communities. When Mayor Bradley responded to the black leadership, the Jewish community was very upset with us because they felt that their point of view was the right one. We still have not picked up our dialogue to the point where we were before. We have a lot of tension in both of these communities. Sometimes people will forget those kinds of issues and sometimes people will *not* forget those kinds of issues.

Your minority community will expect you to go out of your way to do things for them, but there are rules and regulations you have to observe. As I said, it depends upon how you tell them. Do not just tell them, "No, you cannot do it because I am the authority." Learn to explain what the circumstances are. How can they participate? Show them how it can be done and go out of your way to do it.

GOALS FOR THE MINORITY COMMUNITY

My goal with respect to the minority community is to increase their participation at all levels. We are doing very well at the entry levels. We now need to have them filter through to the top so that we can have a pool of people in mid-management that we are able to promote. We need to continue to work on affirmative action and to work against the Reagan administration which is seeking to do away with it.

We need to have minorities participate in the appointment process. I believe we now have thirty Hispanic commissioners, but we really should have more in some of the major departments. We also need to participate in the procurement aspects of the city. We have a small business office that is doing that. We are working with individual departments to make sure that when they send out bids they are sending them to minority and women contractors. This needs to be improved. We are doing much better than we were five years ago, but it is still just a drop in the bucket. We need to have more organizations responding to the bids for service providers to the city. There are many human services that we cannot provide, where we depend on the community, and we need to make sure that we have more of those organizations participating. Mainly, I think my goal for our community is more participation at all levels.

Have I been successful in reaching my goals? I think I have by bringing new people in and by recommending people for appointments. We have a variety of caucuses—black caucuses, Hispanic caucuses, and women's caucuses. I make sure that they are trained, not only that they get together and talk politics, but that they actually get trained in affirmative action, the personnel policies of the city, and the procurement policies of the city, so when they review department policies, they know if they are in compliance and if they are going in the right direction. Therefore, training is very, very important at all levels; and I think that as administrators, we should participate in and initiate various kinds of training programs.

In terms of overall strategies, in keeping with Julian Bond's remarks, I certainly think that we need to stay in front with our civil and human rights movements. We have gotten comfortable over the years because there has been some measure of success for minorities in the United States, but there are always people who are coming behind us. While we may have been successful, I think the political atmosphere in this country is really severely negative. Just to give you an example, The national Civil Rights Commission, through appointments on advisory committees like the one I sit on, is eroding much of the work that was done in the 1960s and 1970s. They are setting us back years and years.

The number of members on these committees used to be set according to the populations of the states. California had twenty-nine members on its committee for years and years. They have cut it down to eleven. Everyone has eleven, regardless of the size of the population. They have wiped out the majority of the people. For instance, within our eleven there are seven Republicans and just four Democrats, and actually one resigned, so there are only three of the old guard that are left. During Ronald Reagan's first administration, they cleaned house and put in a lot of Republicans, but they left the size of the committee at twenty-nine. These Republicans were actually very decent people. They at least believed in civil rights, and although we have had differed on tactics and approaches, we could talk to each other, plan, and study issues.

With the seven that were appointed to this existing committee, there is just absolutely no communication. They are people similar to the character who denied being Hispanic in a book written by Richard Rodriguez. They are of that mentality. There is an Asian, a black, and a Hispanic from the Claremont Colleges, and to a person they say affirmative action never helped them. They absolutely deny it, and they do not want to be referred to as Asian, Hispanic, or black. They could not be anything else, but that is beside the point.

They are initiating studies of affirmative action that deny the fact that there has been any merit to it, and we spend all of our meetings discussing this issue. It is very hard to go to those meetings because you know they will not be productive, they are tension-producing, and you spend all of your time arguing. So I feel very strongly that we need to become more and more aware of this shift and try to achieve greater power and representation at every level of government.

Educational opportunities absolutely have to be pursued, because without an education you are not mobile anywhere. I mean you just are not going to make it. You are not going to have the decent jobs and certainly you are not going to move through career channels without an education. We have to be concerned about all those little kids who are in school now.

I once saw a map of the Los Angeles Unified School District and they had the reading scores outlined according to the schools. It was incredible because you saw all these little dots over here and there was a line across for the national average. All the little dots over here just happened to be all minority schools and, of course, the scattered ones over here that were above the national average were the white schools. You did not need to prove anything else, just look at the reading scores. The illiteracy is not just hitting minority children. We have children across the nation who are not reading and that means that the people who are going to be running this nation are going to be those people who are really not very good readers or writers, or who are not able to understand or verbalize in order to be able to relate to the rest of the world.

I think you always have to respect the possible use of a militant approach to the solution of problems. We are still having demonstrations. In fact, the other day we had a demonstration at city hall on the Gramm-Rudman issue, and we all participated. It reminded me of the sixties—when we all used to get together at the federal building. I think that it is important for professional people to support those kinds of demonstrations as long as they stay peaceful. They will stay peaceful as long as we acknowledge the fact that participants have a very high degree of frustration, which is why they have taken to the streets. Remember that we go home from a job to dinner on our table, whereas many of those people who demonstrate do not. They are homeless, they do not have the money to continue their education, they do not have jobs. There are many reasons why they have such a high frustration level. You cannot ignore the problems because they just fester. It is important for us to acknowledge the fact that there is validity to their frustration and to do what we can to assist them in trying to overcome that frustration.

When I worked for the federal government, I used to walk in many of the demonstrations on the street because I wanted authorities to see that it was not just them, that it was all of us that are impacted. You know it eventually gets to you. You cannot be in that ivory tower all alone.

I would be hesitant in trying to come up with more innovative approaches that have already been set in motion to promote changes in America by the legions of civil and human rights activists over the years. Having been an active participant in the political struggle to achieve greater opportunities for minority Americans, I would continue to counsel that we strive for greater political power and representativeness at every level of government.

We must continue the "full court press" on every front whether it be affirmative action, educational opportunity programs at our colleges and universities for our youths, the fight for more equitable education policies and certainly bilingual education, inclusion of minority Americans on corporate boards, and the whole host of struggles that may vary from community to community. Whether we are talking about protest politics of confrontation or of grass roots persons, who hopefully will not be bought out on compromises, the minority community must continually take assertive and direct action, not to mention well-publicized efforts, to bring about changes.

I must add at this point that militant action in pursuit of a given goal should be interpreted as committed, resourceful, and unwavering devotion to a cause—but not violence. My personal philosophy is certainly that of Cesar Chavez, Martin Luther King, Jr., and the great leaders of history who have advocated a nonviolent assertive approach in their efforts to bring about change. Although violence may grow out of a people's frustration, I often feel that more often than not in the great protests of recent times it has been shown that the protestors have been the victims and not the perpetrators of violent action. I was and am sure many of you were moved by the nonviolent revolution of the Filipino people in Manila a few short weeks ago. I cannot think of a more dramatic illustration of nonviolence than to see the humanity that kneeled before the tanks of the Marcos regime. That protest undoubtedly led to the dissolution of that government. For my part, I feel that violence can be justified when every remedy has been exhausted in the defense of a community's or a person's efforts in defending their rights. I would hasten to add that seldom in our nation's history have we seen a circumstance where violence was a necessary tool utilized by a responsible organization to achieve a lawful right sought by a community of interest.

UNIQUE PROBLEMS/OPPORTUNITIES DUE TO MINORITY STATUS

One of the problems that I am living with now is that the other deputy mayors and I have different agendas. I have looked at my position as one that I would really like to keep as long as possible and, of course, I will be there as long as Tom Bradley is there. The reason for my long-range interest in the position is that it has allowed me to do things that would have been totally impossible without the authority of the mayor. When you call and say, "This is the mayor's office," it is just incredible what you can do—not just in the city but elsewhere, too.

The other deputy mayors seem to view the position as a stepping stone to other positions, and so they have not stayed very long. We have had three of them. The deputy mayor that is here now has his own agenda, and, of course, he is very much involved with the mayor's campaign for the governorship. I find that we are off on different planes and it makes it difficult. They are perfectly content to let me do what I am doing, but there are many times when I do not know what is going on.

People expect a deputy mayor to know everything that is happening, and it is impossible, obviously, especially when there are two different agendas. So rather than sit back and complain about it, I have to devise ways of finding out about meetings. It would be very easy for me to say that I am being ignored because I am Hispanic; but that does not get you anywhere. The thing to do is to project yourself into the situations that are happening around you and find out what is occurring. I even go to the mayor and ask him. I get his schedule routinely every day (that is a security item that only goes to certain people) so I can see what else is going on. The mayor never has any problem if I sit in on a meeting if it is about an issue that concerns me or a topic that I want to learn about.

Particularly being a woman *and* a minority, I have observed that you do not have to wear these things on your sleeve. You do not go to meetings intending to demand that the woman's point of view or the Hispanic or black point of view be introduced. You do not deal with it that way. You go in, sit down, and deal with the things that are before you—the budget, the formation of a committee, etc. People expect you to have a position on the representativeness of the process; therefore, anticipate—engage in anticipatory planning. For instance, in the budget, when we were cutting back in recreation, park, and library services, people just tended to look at the numbers, not from the viewpoint of which community that library is in or what community that library serves. Those kinds of questions are very important and are the kinds of thing that a woman and a mother or a sensitive person (it could be a man) will bring to these kinds of deliberations. You will say, look, that particular area has a high drop-out rate, has a lot of little children just starting kindergarten, has overcrowded schools, year-round schools, or whatever, because you know the community. This then becomes another factor in the deliberations, so that rather than just cutting their services because you are trying to save money, you begin to look at the service and the impact the cuts may have on the community. It is because of sensitivity that you raise the issue in ways that it becomes a question of policy to look at all libraries in terms of effects on people.

If the formation of groups is the issue, then you have to be able to produce the names of blacks and Hispanics to fill the posts, and believe me, that is one of my biggest chores. It is not because the people are not out there, but you always tend to think of the busiest people who are already appointees on other commissions. Therefore, one of the things you might do is develop a pool of resumes, and if you do not appoint them to this one, keep them in mind because you might want to recommend them for something else.

I find also that you do not want to develop the reputation of always going in with the "minority/woman thing." You have to have credibility with the people you work with, that you have something to contribute as an administrator, and have a reputation for getting things done. You have to be concerned about the impact of decisions and build a reputation for being concerned. That is one thing that I have developed. The departments know that I will not support something unless I know how it is going to impact on them; and I will hold up a project until I know. For instance, I've talked to Planning about child care policy when they wanted to establish a position within the planning department to deal with developers, with child care centers. Well, that would not be very economical because how often does somebody come in and want to set up a child care center. So by going to Planning, we decided we could train the existing personnel to respond to those questions rather than establish a separate position.

I do feel that I have many opportunities, but I cannot wait for somebody to say, "I want your input on policy on this issue." You have to take the initiative. You have to do the homework. You have to speak up. However, you do not always have to say, "Hey, I think this is what has to be done." You can ask a question or ask to be a part of the study group so that you are there at the detailed discussions of the issues. Then you can have some input. There are many, many ways to do it, but I think it is wrong when you keep quiet and do not participate.

When I was first appointed, the mayor had what we call a cabinet meeting of all the general managers. It is generally held once a month to discuss policy or any issues that are impacting the departments. It is my job to set up the agenda and send out the notices for the meeting.

The very first meeting we had only two women general managers (we now have three); but I thought, "What in the world am I doing here? I don't know anything about these departments and how they function. What am I going to do? These men must think I'm pretty silly to stand up there and tell them, 'This is what we're going to discuss.' " But then I thought, "My God, I'm deputy mayor and I'm here because of the mayor and this is the mayor's meeting. And so what am I afraid of?" Although my knees were shaking, I soon got over that because the position has the authority, not me; it is the position and it is the mayor's authority that is being projected. I have been doing this for ten years and I have no problems. In fact, I have developed a very good rapport with all the managers. I don't hit them on the head. Rather, I try to work with them and have them support the things that I am doing.

As a woman, let me say a couple of things. The managers developed a wait-and-see policy the first time I ever had to deal with them. Because I am always prepared (and if I am not, I usually have to have a good reason why) and honest with them, they have accepted the fact that I am a minority female. I have a great deal of respect from both the council members and department managers. You just have to prove you can do the job. I have worked hard to change the impression people have of the responsibilities of the deputy mayor. When people realized that it was a woman deputy mayor, they assumed that I was going to be the social secretary. I said, "No, I don't have anything to do with that." At my press conference I made it a point of saying that I was going to do my darndest to be a good administrator because I wanted to keep the door open so that, when I leave, another woman or Hispanic could come in because one Hispanic woman had done a good job.

Having the support of women, I can always call on them to help me and they will be responsive. I also network a lot, particularly with other women. One of the biggest departments we have is general services, which is headed by a woman. If she has problems, she will call me and I will do everything to help her look good—and she will do the same for me. For instance, she is in charge of all the facilities. We have three major buildings in city hall which we outgrew a long time ago. So she has generated a request to look at some of the other nearby buildings that we could buy. I read the report and made sure that the mayor had seen it. One day I was going with the mayor to the produce market and we went by the buildings that were in the report. So I asked the driver to slow down while I pointed them out to the mayor and reiterated to him some of the information from the report so that he could see it. As a result, he is favorably inclined to go along with the purchases. That is an example of the kind of behind-the-scene work you can do.

4

San Diego: Managing in a Conservative Environment

Sylvester Murray

INTRODUCTION

I am city manager for the city of San Diego, California's second largest city. With one million residents, San Diego is the largest city in the United States with a council-manager form of government. Our population contains 15 percent Hispanics, 9 percent blacks, and 2 percent Asians. Twenty-five years from now we expect that 20 percent of the population will be Asian, about 18 to 20 percent will be Hispanic, and about 10 to 12 percent will be black. San Diego will still contain a lot of minorities, but the minority composition will be different—with Asians comprising a much greater proportion of the minority population.

The city has about 7,500 employees. We are—I say this from a point of view of explaining, not complimenting—a conservative Republican city. We are the home of Ed Meese, attorney general, and we were the home of Clarence Pendleton, chairman of the U.S. Civil Rights Commission. We are also the home of Dr. Seuss, for any of you who might have children. So there is a liberal part to us, as well.

In San Diego there is a mayor and eight council members. The mayor is elected at-large. The council members must live in a district. They run in a district primary but then the general election is at-large, so two people from each district run and everybody in the city votes on them.

I am willing to accept council leadership, so I do not have a lot of problems that I know other city managers do. But I also feel it is my obligation to help the council decide policy, and I have determined that the way you do that is much more important than what I propose. So I never get up in a city council meeting and say, "Hey, I'm the city manager. That's my responsibility." I do not have to do that. If they have an issue, then I try to deal with the issue. If they have an issue they want to get passed, if it is something that should not be passed in my opinion, then I try to talk them out of it. But I do not put their backs up against the wall. If you do that, they will look wimpish if they back down. If they do not back down, they will show disrespect for the council-manager form of government. I do not put their backs up against the wall like that. I let them know very clearly that this is not the way I would like to have it done, and invariably they help me at that point by saying, "Well, we'll study it another week. Let's get some more information. Give us a chance to get out from under the television cameras and talk about it." And as a result, I have been able to work very well with councils wherever I have been. Now there have been confrontations at times when I just say, "This is the way I see it and that's it."

ADMINISTRATIVE PHILOSOPHY

I am a manager and always look at management and my definition of management is the *effective manipulation of people and money*. Some of you say, "Oooo, that sounds bad." That is because you think the term "manipulation" is bad. It is not. Manipulate means that you do things in such a way that they come out the way you want them to come out. That is what "manipulate" means. It is not bad. And effective—as opposed to efficient—means the result is good, the value judgment is positive. And people and money is what management is about. You cannot do things without people and, invariably, you have got to have money as a resource also. You motivate people by recognizing them as individuals. You remember people individually; you treat them as people and not as employees.

City managers generally have a lot of policy-making discretion because: (1) their opinion is always asked for, and (2) the administrator usually provides the information needed to make policy. The administrator can also discreetly talk with influential people in the community to plant ideas or to ask them to surface policy positions. This discretion is used when it is politically wise to do so, or when the administrator wants to seem impartial.

INNOVATIONS AND SUCCESSES

Outsiders often measure success by peer acceptance. From a point of view of peer acceptance, I have been elected by my peers as president of the International City Managers Association. I think that is a significant recognition by my peers that I'm a good city manager and a success.

SAN DIEGO

Now that is the second time around. The first time I lost the election. I also have been elected by a larger group of people, including city managers and professors and public administrators, as president of the American Society of Public Administration. That is a recognition beyond just the city managers. I have been awarded the public service award, which means that a group of qualified people sat down and specifically reviewed and said, "He deserves it as opposed to somebody else." I have received a number of other awards, as well, from service groups and organizations. If you are talking about recognition, I have received tremendous recognition. I have been chairman of the Conference of Minority Public Administrators, so that minorities in the profession have recognized me. I look at those as successes.

Professionally, in my first job as the head of the building department in Daytona Beach, I successfully challenged corruption from Mafia and Teamsters' money being used to get hotels built that did not meet building codes, and corruption by developers and zoning lawyers. When I first went there, the developers used to actually bring liquor for the Christmas party to the building department.

In my first job as city manager in Inkster, Michigan, the success was purely concrete. I paved streets that had not been paved in years, and we got houses demolished that should have been demolished a long time ago. One of the most successful programs, which the people of Inkster still love, provided free paint. That idea stemmed from one of those Model Cities programs which had some money. We just announced that if anyone wished to paint a house, we would provide free paint. I also got the city publicly recognized. Some thought Inkster was just a poor black community, but by the time I left, the city was being recognized as a professional community worthy of respect. The proof of that is when I went there to be a city manager, the applications they got for the city manager's job were so unsatisfactory that they called me to come in. When I left, they had about three dozen good city manager applicants.

You can share your successes, because they both make you feel good and they can give somebody else an opportunity to say, "Maybe I'll just do that." Well, what advantage is discussion of failures going to be to you? When you go out for interviews, they are going to ask you: "What are your strong points?" Then they are going to ask you: "What are your weak points?" What are you supposed to stay? If you say, "I don't have any," they say, "You are stuck up." So, when they ask me, "What are your weak points?" I say, "I get agitated sometimes too quickly when I'm dealing with dumb people. And I think that's a weak point because I should be a little bit more giving." It is said in such a way that that person thinks that he is dumb for asking me.

In terms of failures, I did not become president of the City Managers Association the first year that I ran, and you can call that a failure. The system for selecting presidents of the association up until that time included a committee that nominated a person and the association almost invariably voted for the person nominated. It came time for me and the system nominated me. Another guy put out a petition to run and the system allowed the petition. Then he sent out letters to people asking them to vote for him, and he won. It was all right. Then I won the next year.

Among various specific management successes, I introduced strategic planning in Cincinnati and supported management by objectives in Ann Arbor. In both cases the cities were experiencing financial difficulties and it was necessary for us really to plan and justify our activities. I also used these means as tools to get the elected city councils and appointed officials to understand and communicate with each other.

PREPARATION AND LESSONS LEARNED

I got interested in city management as a junior in college. I was born and raised in Miami, Florida. Miami has a council-manager form of government. Dade County, Florida, has a council-manager form of government. Both of them are very well known. I finished in a high school class of 580 people, and I was number ten. So I was kind of smart, but I did not know there was such a thing as a council-manager form of government when I finished high school. All our civics classes taught us about was the federal government. We learned the executive branch, the judicial branch, and the legislative branch. We did not learn about local government. I got interested in local government and was able to get a fellowship/scholarship to go to the University of Pennsylvania for a program in governmental administration.

At the University of Pennsylvania, the Fels Institute was a part of the Wharton School, and we were required to take all core courses that a person going for a master's in business administration would take. I did not have all of those core courses, so even though I had finished the Fels program they would not give me the degree until I had taken the remaining core courses. I did not look at that as being very important and I ended up working. I got drafted during the Vietnam War. It was after all of that happened that I took the final courses, so I got the degree in 1967. All of my classmates finished in 1964.

At Fels, there were twenty-five of us in the class. The professor got in front of a class one day and said (and I was the only black in the class) to everybody there, "All of you will be city managers in five years after you finish here if you would like, except you, Sy." He said it in front of the class. He said, "We have to acknowledge that you are black, and American cities will never have a black city manager, but if you do well you can still get a good job because we had another black who came through this program about ten years ago and he is now a professor at

Morgan State. So you can do that." I felt very bad but I did not cry in that class and I did not cry outside of class. Instead, what I did was simply to acknowledge what the man was telling me. This was before the 1964 Civil Rights Act, this was before Martin Luther King. He said I was not going to be able to make it like these other guys in the class. I accepted that, recognized that I was black, and gave myself seven years to do what they were going to do in five (saying I would take two more years for being black). I would try it and if I was not a city manager in seven years, and these white boys in this class were, then I would get out and go teach school." I did make it. My first job was in 1970. Between 1964 and 1970, I put two years in the army. I made it within my seven. That was the only thing that was important to me.

In another instance at the university, we had to write a thesis. The thesis had to be finished in about eighteen months. At Christmas time, when my professor called me in to look at my paper, he said to me, "Your paper is a potpourri of nothing." He told me, in essence, that when everybody else was going to rest during Christmas, "Now, over the holidays you can start all over again from scratch and come back with the paper at the level that everybody had four months to bring it to, or you cannot come back." That was the only black professor I had at the university. I looked at the professor and I said, "Is that all?" He said, "Yes." And I left him.

You will be discouraged in your career by a lot of people, and especially by people that you do *not* think you will be discouraged by, especially if you are a minority. It is very important when that happens that you still know what you are about and that you do not hold it, necessarily, against that person. I mean I still know the professor, but the point was, I did not have to say to him, "Why are you doing this to me?" I also did not come up and say, "I'll be back and I'll have the paper ready." I was not certain that I would, because I was going home for vacation. I did revise the paper and it turned out okay. If you go back and look at the record, I did not get an *A* on it; I do not even know if I got a *B* but it passed. I gave him what he wanted.

The third kind of experience that I had a Fels, memorably, was with another one of the professors. This professor was very concerned about our careers and he would say to us as youngsters, "if you want to be a city manager, your personal life is much more important than just knowing the subject. Your wife is important." He had a party at his house so that we could invite our wives or our girlfriends, and he would give us an assessment if that was the right woman for our careers. If you did not come to the party, you could not get an *A* out of his class. So everybody went to the party. I took with me to the party one of the nicest whores Philadelphia had. Deliberately. He said she was okay.

You ought to like yourself, and I have met people who really do not like themselves. I have met people who dislike themselves so much that, when they brush their teeth in the morning, they do not look in the mirror. That is right. They are standing right there at the sink, where there is a mirror in front of them, but when they brush their teeth they put their head down so they will not see themselves in the mirror. Brush your teeth looking at yourself saying at the same time, "I like what I see." Keep saying that because it is important.

People always ask if there were experiences in my childhood that prepared me for my current profession. Let me give you my facetious answer first. When I was growing up in Miami, Florida, I lived in Liberty City, and those of you who are old enough know that is where the riots were. It is right outside the city limits. When we were growing up, the sheriff would come by. We even had black deputy sheriffs at that time. But whether they were black or white, as children, we used to run from them, scared, because we had seen the police with their nightsticks beat people up. So we were scared of the police. I never forgot that and when in college it was explained to me what a city manager was and told that if you were city manager you were boss of the police, I said, "Damn, that's the job I want. That's my job!" That is the facetious one.

In all seriousness, the things in my background that really helped were the training I got at Fels and the sense of liking people and working with people. If you do not like people, this is just the wrong kind of profession to be in. And many get in our profession who do not like people. They believe, if you are in charge of garbage collection, all you have to do is make certain that the garbage is collected. And a lot of things are lost. I think that government is service to people.

I have been city manager of San Diego for six months or so. Before San Diego, I was city manager for Cincinnati for six years; before Cincinnati, I was city manager of Ann Arbor, Michigan, for six years; and before Ann Arbor, I was city manager of Inkster, Michigan, for three years. Inkster is a little community that sits between Detroit and Ann Arbor. So I am in my fourth city-manager city and the term "six" has meaning to me. Even though we move a lot, we set as a special goal that I would not move while my children were in school. So the six had meaning. It allowed my oldest daughter to be six years from the first grade to the sixth in one city in one house, and to be from seventh grade to graduation in one city in one house.

I left Inkster after just three years because my daughter was beginning first grade and the school system in Inkster was not that good. So I knew while she was only three that when she became six years old I wanted her to be in a good public school system because I was not able to send her to private school.

I have been lucky that the right kinds of jobs came open at the time I was looking for them. But I was willing to say to you on an informal

SAN DIEGO

basis that if it was not the right kind of job, I probably would have gone to a lesser job because it was the time for me to do it. On the assumption that very few city managers can stay in one city for twelve years, I knew that there would have to be a change.

I chose city management. Let me go back and say why I got to San Diego. I got to San Diego not as a part of a plan, I will admit that. My daughter started college, so I did not have to worry about her being uprooted. I have a son and I have been divorced for about two years, and my son is with his mother. So that did not have an impact. I got to San Diego solely because they asked me to come, and I was not looking for a job.

During graduate school, I had several other experiences that occurred because I was black. Fels had internship programs. As part of the internship, you would be paid $200 a month. You got a grade at the end of the period. The director of the school liked me. He was the one who encouraged me to go there, and he found a place for me to intern. They have this little network on the Philadelphia Mainline. I said to the director, "I'd like to go back to Miami because now I know that they have a city manager system. I would like to go back home to intern." He said, "Well, we don't have one down there for you. You have to go out to a Philadelphia suburban area." I said, "I want to go back and intern because I cannot live on $200 a month in a Philadelphia suburb." So he said, "Okay, Sy, since you are so adamant, you go down there and try to get an internship yourself."

I did. I went down and talked with the assistant city manager to ask him for an internship. The assistant city manager was a man who finished the same program at Fels that I did five years before. He was white. And he told me, "No." Then I told him about coming from Miami and, even though my people were not political, a lot of white folks do not know if they are or not, so I gave the impression that they were. They might have been political in the black part of town. He came back and said to me, "Okay, we'll give you an internship at a recreation center in the black neighborhood." I wanted to be a city manager and he was going to give me an internship in the recreation center in the black neighborhood. I said to him, "No, no, thank you. I want an internship like you had in the city manager's office, and if it's not in the city manager's office and it's in the recreation department, I want it to be in the *headquarters* of the recreation department. He said, "That's not what I'm offering you." So I said, "No."

Then I dutifully called the director back and said, "You won. I lost. I cannot get an internship down here." So that is my next lesson for you. When you are looking, admit when you have made an error. It was a mistake for me to think that I could have gotten an appropriate internship in Miami in 1964. I did not know that. I tried it. I did not push it. I did not yell. I just said, "I lost this one. I made a mistake. I should have followed what the director said." Then the director called me and said, "Well, since you were so adamant, I have been looking while you have been gone and we have a position in Daytona Beach, Florida, if you want to go there." So rather than go back to Pennsylvania, I went to Daytona Beach and I got an internship with Norman Hickey, and that is how my career started.

Norman Hickey was a liberal city manager. His assistant city manager, also white, was conservative. When my internship was completed in six months and they were thinking about offering me a job—by this time it was 1965, and the civil rights movement was in full swing—I asked for $100 a week pay. The city manager said, "No, that is too much money." They were paying police officers $77 a week at that time. He said, "That's too much money and we cannot do it." He was getting ready to negotiate with me when his conservative assistant city manager said, "It is worth a hundred dollars a week to us for him to be sitting out front." The city manager turned red. When he got his composure back, I said to him, "The man is right. Pay me the hundred dollars."

As you are developing as a minority public administrator, you are going to encounter many things that appear to be swipes. They are only going to be swipes if you allow them to be. I wanted a hundred dollars. The conservative was willing to pay me the hundred dollars. Now I had not thought about where I was going to sit when I was thinking about how much money I wanted. So that was not a goal; that was insignificant. The hundred dollars is what I wanted, and I was willing to sit out in front if that is what they wanted. But sitting out front worked to my advantage. When you sit out in front, you see what is going on. Even though I did not have any authority, I saw who did have it. I was able to see who really got into the city manager's office and who did not. I was able to see whose phone calls were returned and whose were not, and that has always helped me.

Another experience that may be useful concerns when I got ready to leave Daytona Beach during the Vietnam War. When I was drafted for the war, the city manager came to me and said, "You don't have to go." I was still the only black in city hall except the janitor, and at that time they were getting ready to have riots in Daytona Beach. So essentially what he was saying was, "We can get you off because we need you in the city," for your blackness. He did not say that but I understood it. I said, "No, I will go. I will not volunteer for the war, but if they call me, I will go." So I went.

Some very interesting things happened in the army. I came to the army with a master's degree, but I was, after basic training, assigned to the infantry. Before basic training ended, I did very well as a recruit. The colonel in charge of the company suggested to me that I go to officer's candidate school. I told him, "No, thank you." He said, "But you have the qualifications. You're a leader, Sy. You ought to go to officer's school." I told him, "No, thank you. You know I do not love this army. I am here because you called me." He said, "What are you going to do with your life?" I said, "I am going to be a city manager." He said, "If you really want to be a city manager, go to officer's training school. You can actually get to manage cities as an army officer because you will be places where you're in command, and you can have all those responsibilities." I thought about it and I said, "This sounds right, but that's not the city manager position that I was thinking about. I'm not going to take it." He continuously enticed me and one day we were out on the parade field with all the troops in the battalion and the man called me out: "Murray, here!" in front of all the guys. I went up to the command post and he said to me, "Didn't that make you feel good?" And I said, "What, sir?" "To be recognized by all these people. Everybody knows now that you are special." I said, "Yes, it did." He said, "Go to officer's training school. You are special." And I said to him, "Colonel, if I'm that special, give me a commission now. You have the authority to do it. I do not have to go to officer's training school. Give me the commission and I will stay." He told me, "Get back in the ranks...."

Challenge people if it is necessary. Even though you like yourself, even though you have to follow orders, challenge when it is necessary. I challenged him. Of course, he refused to budge, but he did not bother me anymore. You are going to meet people throughout your career who will always suggest to you that there are certain things you can do that will make it better. When you start working, you will start getting ready for promotions. One thing everybody is going to tell you is, "Go to this training school. Go to this academy. Go to this supervisor's training method. All of that will help you get promoted." I am not telling you not to take training, but I am telling you that sometimes you have to look people in the eye and say, "I am already trained. I am already educated. I have come to you qualified. Now if you really mean business I can be promoted right now to do the job."

After I turned the colonel down, the next thing I knew I got orders to go to the Panama Canal Zone. Maybe because I came from Miami they *thought* I spoke Spanish, but I really did not. So I went to the sergeant and said, "Sergeant, why am I going to the Panama Canal Zone?" He said, "It is not your business. You go wherever the army sends you." I said, "Sergeant, I have been a very good soldier. I would do what the army tells me to do, but I do not intend to go to Vietnam. I really cannot go to Vietnam. That would be a big, big blot in my career goals, and I do not want to go to Panama where they have jungle training for Vietnam. Now, Sergeant, you have been in this man's army for twenty-seven years. You have got to be able to do something to keep me from going to the Panama Canal Zone, and I am asking you outright to do something for me, please. I have been a good soldier, I am going to stay a good soldier for two years, but I need your help *now*. It is very important." The orders for Panama Canal Zone were rescinded, and I was assigned to the staff of a bird colonel in Fort Monroe, Virginia, who was studying for a Ph.D. in political science at George Washington University through a correspondence course. I spent two years in the army writing his papers and being supervisor of the Xerox machine staff of five.

I got promoted just like that. During the war you could get early promotions. In twenty-one months in the army from the day I was drafted to the day I left, I had promotions to sergeant E5. It was as fast as you could go, and then I got an early out. I was supposed to stay twenty-four months, but the colonel was so appreciative of my writing papers for which he was getting a lot of *A*s, he wanted to help me. The way he wanted to help me was a civil service job in Washington, D.C. I told him, "Nope, that is not what I want. If you want to help me, get me out." And he did. The lesson that I am trying to communicate to you is when you want a favor, ask for it. A lot of times you need favors. Do not be ashamed to ask somebody to help you if you really want to be helped and that person has the authority to help you.

When I was in Daytona Beach, I did well. I was promoted from assistant to the city manager to director of the building department. At the end of two years, I learned that I was a real good building department director. You get to be a department head, and you can stay there forever and retire. If you do well, you have authority, a lot of people underneath you, you are respected, and make a lot of money. I was doing very well in my job and in my finances, so I was getting comfortable. At that point, I had forgotten about becoming a city manager. So I thought about it and I realized I would have to leave this job because I was not making progress toward city management. People could not understand why I would quit, but I did not quit before I got another job. I began to plan my career.

I knew that I wanted to be a city manager. I had to be an assistant city manager someplace. People need to see that title behind your name. The title "assistant city manager" was my goal. I did not care what the job description was, I did not care where it was, or who it was with. I wanted the title, "assistant city manager," behind my name. I sent out many applications. One went to a city manager in Illinois. I will never forget this one. I had a beautiful resume. The city manager hired me without a personal interview. He hired me based on the resume, school, and the people he had talked with about me. He called and said, "Now, when you come up for discussion, we are going to introduce you to the city council and have a press conference at the same time, so send a picture." So I sent a picture; I never heard from him again! He did not even call and say, "I'm sorry, I can't do it." He just sent a note and said, "We have run out of money in the budget." You know, you can always say that. I just did not hear from the man anymore. Finally, I called him and the secretary said the job had been filled. I do not know if there is a lesson in that for you, but it made me even more determined to become a city manager.

I made a note that the next city manager's convention that I went to I was going to find that manager, look him in the face and tell him who I was. That is all I wanted to do, and I did it. I went up to him, looked at him, and I said, "I am Sylvester Murray," turned, and left.

Career advancement does not occur by happenstance. I planned my career. I am not saying that I totally controlled it, but I knew what I wanted to happen. The most important advice I can give to you is the importance of being in a position to control your life. Your life is not Calvinistic, your career is not Calvinistic. *You* have some control over what happens in your life and the way you do that may sound simplistic. First, you must identify your career goals. What is it you want to accomplish? You must make the statement and put a deadline on its accomplishment. You have to say what it is you want to do and when you want to have it done.

As minorities, a lot of things are important to career advancement but those things that I think are extremely important, not necessarily in order, are: (1) that you have to like yourself as an individual, and (2) you have to like yourself as a minority. You cannot function well as a minority if you really think you are in a white position. Very, very often, I have heard minorities say, "I have a white man's job." These people are not going to function well because they really do not think that they ought to be doing the job. You have to like yourself as an individual and you have to recognize that if you have a job, that has to be a minority's job when you are in it. If you believe it is a minority occupying a white man's job, you never will function well.

You have to recognize, if you are appointed to your job by white people, they expect you to be a minority when you occupy the job. Very often we forget that and we think that they are appointing us because we are so highly qualified and, as a result, we have to show that qualification by not acting "minority-wise."

People look at you—they see and know that you are different when they appoint you. They know that you are black, they know that you are a woman, they know that you are a minority. If you get in that position and try to act as if you are not, then you are disappointing the people that appointed you. People can only be disappointed when they have expectations. Essentially, what I am saying is that when you get there, you do not have to apologize for what you do, and you have an obligation to do something that is different.

Most people are hired, promoted, and fired because of personality traits, chemistry between two people rather than education, resumes, or degrees. You ought to recognize that. If you are simply in a civil service position and you got the job because you were the top person on the list, then there is no problem. You got that job because you qualified for it. But if you want a job that is going to have a real impact on people and your community, you should be getting a job that is civil service exempt. When you get an exempt job, you are getting that because of personality traits and chemistry. The extent to which you can be effective in that job is also on the basis of personality traits and chemistry.

How do you react to the community? In San Diego, when we say, "the community," we are speaking of the minority community. How do you react to the community when you are appointed to a job that allows you to make a lot more money, to have a title behind your name, and to get newspaper reporters asking you questions? You should react from a point of view of saying, "I like myself." But you should also react from a point of view of saying, "I know I am qualified for the job and I am not just here because I am a minority." Now do not get confused—I said at the beginning that when they appointed you, they knew you were minority. But when you react to that job, your reaction has to be: This is a job that I can totally do. That also becomes important when you are seeking a promotion. Some people may ask if you have had any more training courses or what was the last management course you took. These questions are intended to get you to admit that you are not absolutely qualified. You have to respond that you are here totally prepared; you came trained. You have got to say that you are today totally trained, can teach it to anybody else, and can write the book on the subject.

You must also have a sense of obligation from the point of view of mentoring. There has to be somebody elses in that organization or somebody else close by who wants your job. There is *always* somebody who wants your job. But there ought to be somebody who is a minority who wants your job. Whether that happens depends in large part on how you act in your organization. If no other minority wants that job, then you are not performing well. You have an obligation to recognize that at a certain level, your professionalism goes beyond just your job. If you are involved in staff meetings with chief management officials or you are a part of strategic planning sessions with higher management people, in any way involved in decision-making responsibilities with groups and committees, then you have an obligation to recognize other minorities, not just those in your department, but other people in the organization who have a possibility of being promoted or getting a position. You can be the purchasing director, but you can have an impact on who works in other departments. You do that very easily. You should do that whenever you get the opportunity—make statements that say, "John Jones is a good man. He has his head screwed on right. Susan Smith is a good woman." When you can let somebody in decision-making authority know that somebody else exists out there, then you have an obligation to do so.

Minority administrators must get out into the community and communicate. We can never use as an excuse to any other minority: "I do not understand what you mean. What are you really asking for? What do you want?" You cannot use that as an excuse. You may say, "I am sorry I cannot give you that job. I am sorry I do not think you are ready for this." But you cannot say, "I do not know what it is you are asking for." You must also be human. A lot of minorities simply fail to be courteous to other minorities. You must return phone calls. At minimum, you must speak to them when you are walking down the hallways. You have to be able to say to other minorities, "Not only am I here, not only do I like myself, not only am I good at what I do, but I know you and I like you, too."

Finally, we have to remember that regardless of the position, regardless of the money, regardless of the title, if somebody appointed you to that position, they can take you out of it.

COMMUNITY RELATIONS

Usually my major sources of support have come from white business groups and chamber of commerce types. These majority people have always appreciated my business approach to handling the finances of cities. Major minority support has come from black ministers and self-help neighborhood groups, because I initiated projects that benefit low income groups in cities.

One question your own community will ask is, "What does it mean to us that you are a black? What are you going to do for us?" One question you will have to ask is, "Do you think the questions have any meaning?" The questions have meaning to black folks. The meaning is that you can talk to me and I understand what you are saying. Often, as minorities, when you talk to the people of the majority race, you are not really certain that they understand. You are not really certain that they know what you are talking about, because you are not certain where they are coming from even though you are using the same language. But if you are a minority city manager—say Hispanic—and another Hispanic came up and talked to you, you cannot use as an excuse that he did not explain it right. You cannot use as an excuse that he did not use the right words. That is what I offer to blacks—that I know what it is they are saying. Now from that point on it becomes an issue of whether I can do it or not. But I cannot say I did not know what they were saying.

Minority administrators have a responsibility to advance the hiring of other minorities, but many feel timid about exercising their authority in this area. You have an obligation to deliver. Do you know that when whites hire minorities in positions of authority they expect that minorities are going to deliver to minorities? When a white city manager or a white city council hires a black person and gives him authority to hire, he expects that he is going to hire blacks. They *expect* it, and *we* disappoint them because *we* think that *we* should not show "favoritism!" I am firmly convinced of that. They expect that we are going to be fair to minorities who are like us. Politicians frequently cannot say that the city is going to hire all of these blacks and adhere to strict affirmative action guidelines, but when they hired you they have made a commitment to it. If you have been given the authority to hire and they think that you will hire blacks, then you should get blacks into key positions. If you do not do it, you will disappoint the whites who hired you. I do not disappoint them; I hire blacks and other minorities, too.

The black community expected that when I got in a position to influence the capital improvements budget, I would pave some streets in the black community. When it came time to do the resurfacing, they expected that I would take it on my own initiative to make certain that the black community got their streets resurfaced without them having to write a petition. I did that. The community expects more and you are supposed to deliver. Should you do anything unprofessional? Should you do anything unethical to help black people? No! No! However, if it is not unethical and if it is not unprofessional, you are supposed to do it. And I live by that code.

Let me give you one example. At the time the San Diego fire chief had quit, they were going through the process of hiring a new fire chief. I had been selected to be city manager, and I was in San Diego to look at housing when the acting city manager said, "Well, Mr. Murray, we had already set up a system to replace the fire chief and we have this process. Would you like for us to stop that process until you get here?" I said (which was the right thing to say because it was my appointment), "No, just make certain that there are minorities on the list because we have to be concerned about affirmative action." He said, "Okay." Now what could they say other than that? What I was saying was you can go through and get your list of five candidates but make sure a minority is on the list.

When I got there, they gave me a list of five people. Sure enough, they had a black man on it, and I appointed him as fire chief. He was already in the San Diego Fire Department but was five levels down in the hierarchy. They never expected that I would do that, but they made a mistake of making him the only San Diego person on the list. The other people were apparently more qualified than he. One, in fact, had already been the fire chief in another California city, and they just knew that I was going to go through that list and say, "Well, this guy already has five years experience as a fire chief." From my view, however, the search committee told me that all five candidates on this list were qualified, and I could make any selection I wanted. I believe in homegrown talent, so I appointed the black guy. The council got a little angry that I did not discuss it with them—but I did it.

I sat down and talked with the new chief the day I made the decision. I told him, "Now look, we have an 800-man fire department, and since only 40 of them are black, you have an obligation. I do not have to set down any affirmative action rules for you. I do not have to send you any management letters. If you are appointed the fire chief here, you have an obligation. Do you understand that?" He said, "Of course, Mr. Murray, of course."

Sometimes there has been tension as a result of my affirmative action views. For example, the police and fire unions in Cincinnati created tension because they felt my position on affirmative action in hiring and promoting in the uniformed services was too one-sided.

I serve as a spokesperson for minority interests. I do it publicly when advocating special social/economic programs for a city. I also do it behind the scenes with businessmen and special groups who want counsel but do not want publicity. I have done so to suggest that minorities should be appointed to special committees and task forces. I have also worked with newspaper editors to suggest minority news coverage.

GOALS FOR THE MINORITY COMMUNITY

I do not have a particular goal with respect to the minority community goal, thus I am not working towards something happening at a certain time. I have tried to go everywhere somebody asks me to go, so that they can see a black city manager. I have tried to use myself as a symbol, so that when I see minorities, even though I cannot help them directly, at least if they ask, "Can I get a job?" I can give them the information. Then I like to just let people see me, to see that I am a city manager and have been in the profession a long time.

As president of the American Society for Public Administration, I will certainly work to improve the situation of minorities in the profession. I have worked with the International City Managers Association to set up special recruitment offices within the agency so that we have a list of all qualified people. When cities start looking for city managers, we send them names of qualified minorities so that it is impossible for them to say, "We cannot find anybody qualified."

Whenever I leave a city, it has more blacks and more minorities, and even more women in management positions than when I was hired. I say that a little bit reluctantly because I am biased, and I think that you can get just as many brownie points for being a woman as you get for being a minority; and that is not fair. But I do make an effort to hire white women.

There are various ways that minorities can work to meet their goals. I do not believe in violence, but there is a role for peaceful protest, however. Marches, petitions, speeches, and nonviolent confrontations are very legitimate means for minorities to promote and demand change. I support such actions.

UNIQUE PROBLEMS/OPPORTUNITIES DUE TO MINORITY STATUS

It is an advantage to be a minority, and there is a special relationship. I am black. There is no doubt about it. I cannot pass for white. Let me give you a couple of instances in terms of relationships. When I went to Ann Arbor, one of the first meetings I went to was with a group of police offiers. All were white, except for one black sergeant in the room whom I did not even notice because the place was filled with white officers. When it came to the question and answer session, this big white officer stood up in the back of the room and said, "I want to know if you are going to be a black city manager or a city manager who happens to be black." I stood up so as not to be nervous and walked back there where he was. It was important that I do that. I walked back there where I could face him and I said, "I am a black city manager. I was born black. I did not have a choice. I could have happened to be a lawyer. I could have happened to be a teacher, but I happen to be a city manager. I did not happen to be black. That makes me a black city manager, not a city manager who happens to be black."

I walked back to the front of the room, glad that my knees held out while I was standing up there. "Now," I said to him, "you know what you really were asking me? You were asking me: Because I am black, which you recognized when you asked the question, am I going to treat you any differently or am I going to treat you unfairly because you are white? That is what you were asking me. As a black city manager, am I going to treat you, a white police officer, unfairly? You were not even concerned if I would treat the black police officer with favoritism. What you were concerned about is that I not treat you unfairly, and I will not."

5

Seattle: Providing Health Care for an Invisible Population

JoAnn Kauffman

INTRODUCTION

I am executive director of the Seattle Indian Health Board, and we are one of those thousands of small nonprofit programs trying to meet human resource needs. The Seattle Indian Health Board, incorporated in 1970, provides volunteer services—volunteer doctors and nurses—to take care of Indians who need health care. We employ over one hundred professionals and paraprofessionals who provide health services for roughly 90 percent of all the Indians and Alaskan natives who live in the Seattle–King County area—about 20,000 individuals.

Many times Indian and Alaskan Native people, especially in the larger cities, become invisible to the rest of the population. But the Indian population has unique health care needs and problems. For example, the causes of death for Indian people are totally different than the causes of death for the general public. In fact, five of the top ten leading causes of death for Indian people are alcohol related. If the health care system were established only for the general population, it is highly unlikely that the system would be able to adequately address and meet the needs of a subpopulation with needs as different as an Indian population.

There are also cultural barriers that inhibit the participation of distinct groups such as American Indian people in systems designed for the general public, for example, the numerous community health centers throughout the United States. In the Seattle area, we surveyed community mental health centers to determine how many Indian people were using their services. Many reported that no Indian people were utilizing their facilities for mental health counselling, and those who did report some contact with Indian people indicated they came only once and did not return for follow-up visits.

Our position—that services for Indian people must be offered in a way that is sensitive to their culture—has proven to be valuable in providing mental health services. We now furnish over 90 percent of all the mental health, medical, dental, and alcoholism treatment services for Indian people in the Seattle area, that is, for virtually *all* the Indian people in the Seattle–King County area. Thus, by providing care for 90 percent of this population, we are a vital link to the community even though we are not formally within the structure of the local government. If we were eliminated, there would be a gap in service delivery for a population in grave need.

ORGANIZATION

With over one hundred staff and a $3.5 million budget, we have one of the largest nonprofit community health centers in our area. The board of directors is the legal entity of the nonprofit corporation, and it is composed of a group of volunteer citizens who meet at least monthly. They hire the executive director, and I, in turn, supervise the heads of each of the departments, who supervise the care givers. My responsibilities involve the direct administration of the organization, but also extend out into the community by networking with local government, serving as an advocate to improve health and social services to the Indian population, and working as a team member with other minority representatives from the city of Seattle to help improve services for the minority population.

When I was hired as executive director in 1982, I left the Northern Idaho Tribes. I became familiar with the job and organization when I worked as a grant writer. I knew it would be a challenge. The policies of the Reagan administration had begun to take effect. The cutbacks in Indian health services and the threatened elimination of other health care resources, such as women's, infant and children's nutrition programs, family planning, and numerous other programs which provided services for low-income people, were all under the threat of elimination because of policy and philosophical changes at the federal level.

The Seattle Indian Health Board was to be eliminated during the 1982 funding cycle, and the staff's morale was low. To compound the problems, the organization had moved out of a building for which it had signed a long-term lease, thereby breaking a contract. Rightfully, the landlord filed suit against the organization. The board's financial management had been suffering for years prior to my arrival, and it had just gone through an audit that indicated that not all of the funds were accounted for. Thus, it was a very dismal situation.

I was not really aware of the financial status of the agency through the interview process, but within hours of arriving I began to find that each day would be a new adventure. It has been my most challenging job, and I often reflect back to the training I had at the School of Public Health at the University of California, Berkeley. It is difficult to take what you learned about the external and internal environments and management and try to talk to people who are literally weeping at the staff meeting. In desperation, they would say, "Let's just shut the place down. Let's plan for an orderly phaseout. Let's stop kidding ourselves. This agency isn't going to make it. The books are all screwed up. We're not going to get any money until October 1. My wife and I just bought a house. This is it. I need to find another job." It was very difficult, to say the least.

REBUILDING

The first six months at the Seattle Indian Health Board were the most crucial. There were many things that happened during that time that I would like to share with you, particularly those of you who might be working in a situation where an agency might be teetering on catastrophe or dying a slow death. Some of what I did might be helpful to you.

One of my first efforts was to take an inventory of the damage and ask for an audit of the agency to establish a beginning point for a new administration and a cutoff from an old administration. I would recommend that whenever you enter an agency that has gone through turmoil, whether it is a private, freestanding organization or a nonprofit—establishing a time line is important. My next step was to identify a broad coalition of supporters for the organization. We had a coalition made up of people from the mayor's office, the Council of Churches, the AFL-CIO, hospital administrators, other community clinics, other minority agencies—just anyone that we could think of who might be somewhat sympathetic. We called it the "Coalition to Save the Seattle Indian Health Board." We were very fortunate because the changes brought about by the new Reagan administration had generated a lot of interest in what was going to happen to the Seattle Indian Health Board. The Public Health Hospital in the Seattle area had almost been eliminated, some people were sensitized to the issues.

The next step was to educate as many people as possible. I developed "care" packages for anybody who wanted to know anything about the agency or the coalition. At that time, the Seattle Indian Health Board did not have a lot of good print. One of the things we did was to call a press conference to announce the formation of the coalition, tell people that the Seattle Indian Health Board might be closed, and inform them that 20,000 Indians were not going to have any place to receive their health care. The press came and took pictures of the clinic and people being seen by the doctor. We distributed the names of important persons on the coalition list. The most significant factor about the newspaper article on the organization was not that it appeared in a newspaper, but making a hundred copies of it and using them as publicity was the greatest value of getting the news article. The copies were useful when we sought to expand the support network to another level.

These kinds of activities were very critical in developing political support, and the Seattle community became much stronger during that first year. People went from the mind-set of, "Well, gee, there's another nonprofit that isn't going to make it through the transition years," to "There's no way we can let this agency fold because of the importance of health care for Seattle Indians." They knew the statistics. If 20,000 Indians are not served by the Seattle Indian Health Board, where were they going to go? The hospitals would lose millions of dollars if 20,000 people started to show up in the emergency rooms.

Other problems centered around building employee morale, and it is a problem that still continues today. As a nonprofit organization, funding is really contingent upon annual appropriations made through a variety of governmental levels, but, primarily, the federal level. Consequently, given the Reagan administration, employee morale has been difficult. We have dealt with it by sponsoring events and providing time off for employees. We take one day every quarter for everybody to get together aside from regular staff meetings and have special in-service training time—so people get to know each other. To start rewarding people for extraordinary service, we hold an annual event that recognizes the overall mission of the organization. Presumably, people are not just there because it is a job, but because there is a purpose for this agency—and that purpose is Indian health care. Therefore, we began an annual recognition for personnel who have made outstanding contributions to Indian health, either inside or outside of the agency. It has been a slow but successful process.

In the first six months, we were able to clean up the books and have a clean audit at the end of the calendar year. We managed to pull together political support to make the continuation of the board an important issue and to boost morale. It took several years to settle the suit that resulted when the agency had to move out of leased quarters. The suit was the final skeleton that I was handed when I came in in 1982, and it finally has been put to rest.

MOVING AHEAD

Today we are still not absolutely sure, especially with the Gramm-Rudman uncertainties, what our funding situation is going to be like at the beginning of the next fiscal year. But we do know that we have a lot of support and that the staff involved at the Seattle Indian Health Board can read the newspapers and can ask questions about how this might affect their job or our agency. We are looking ahead. We celebrated our fifteenth anniversary this past year and spent a lot of time talking about how to observe the event. Between the staff and board, we decided that the anniversary would be a dedication to future directions rather than a reflection on accomplishments from the first fifteen years. Therefore, the anniversary was dedicated to a very ambitious goal: the elimination of Indian alcoholism in our lifetime. But this new commitment has made a real change in how people perceive their jobs and their roles in the organization. We are not simply employees who show up to deal with a crabby supervisor or complain about small benefits and low pay. We are there because we are involved in a mission. This agency wants to make a difference, wants to make a change, and I am a very important piece of it regardless of whether I am the person who greets the patient at the front desk or the counselor who finally gets someone into inpatient treatment for alcoholism.

I would like to summarize by saying that my position with the Seattle Indian Health Board has been a real opportunity. When somebody told me that the Chinese symbols for crises were translated literally as "opportunity riding on the dangerous wind," I wrote it down and stuck it on the wall by my desk. I have looked at it a number of times because it really is an opportunity for change, an opportunity to get people involved. As executive director for the Seattle Indian Health Board, I was handed a crisis which provided me an opportunity to educate people in Seattle about what we do and the problems of Indian health. Moreover, it has also been a very important opportunity for community individuals to become involved in saving a very important community service.

ADMINISTRATIVE PHILOSOPHY

My philosophy today is one of involvement. I heard somebody once refer to a style called MBWA, Management by Wandering Around. I liked the way that sounded because there is something about knowing who the people are that work for you by name or introducing yourself to new employees, talking about where you came from and have you found a place to live, or things of that nature that are important. Having a good understanding of what is happening in each of the departments or each of the functions of my supervisors is also important. There was a time when accounting and finance matters were a mental block for me, so my philosophy was to hire somebody to do that and let me know when it was done. That does not really work. You have to sit down and try to learn those areas you do not understand so that you can carry on an intelligent conversation and know how each unit is performing. I also emphasize openness. That is something that I have tried to do without circumventing the structure of supervisors and department heads. It is still important to hear people's perceptions about what they think, how they think things ought to be run. My style has been one of participation—involvement in trying to know people.

In 1983 we started the employee of the year awards which are determined by the employees. Nominations come from the employees and the board picks six people. Each December we have our annual all-day staff meeting. We conduct business in the morning and have a potluck Christmas party and gift exchange in the afternoon. The employee of the year is announced during the party and everybody who was nominated gets a certificate. It is meaningful and appreciated by the employees because they know it is not one person who is bestowing the award, but their fellow workers have nominated them. Each nominee gets a certificate and the six people who had the most votes each get a certificate, plus a small gift, plus a day off. It is not very expensive to do, but it has made a big difference to our employees. About September or November they start asking, "Where are the ballots? Where are the ballots?" It is an emotional and exciting time.

I have policy-making discretion within the boundaries set by my board of directors. The board reserves the right to approve and disapprove such things as our annual budget, five-year plan, patient quality assurance plans, patient grievance procedures, personnel policies and contractual obligations, excluding personnel, which exceeds $10,000 per year. As the CEO, I can interpret these policies and set administrative policy on services, staff, and outside affiliations.

INNOVATIONS AND SUCCESSES

About a year and a half ago, we made the decision to seek accreditation by the Joint Commission for the Accreditation of Hospitals (JCAH). They have recently begun accrediting outpatient programs. There was discussion that we would no longer be eligible to receive Medicare and Medicaid payment if we were not JCAH accredited. Since this is a nationally-accepted standard of quality that everybody accepts, at least at the hospital level, we wanted to be accredited. That was the easy decision. But when we got the manual in the mail about the accreditation process and the check list of things that had to be undertaken, we realized we had a lot of work ahead of us. The whole organization had to be divided into different functional components, and each functional component had a list of criteria that had to be met. Each individual went through the checklist and took an inventory of what we were doing right and what we were doing wrong. It was such an enormous undertaking that no one person could do it alone. The process, however, was very good for the morale of the agency, because it meant that everybody had to be a participant.

People were given areas of responsibility, e.g., the safety committee, the facility committee, the quality assurance committee. All of those different pieces had to have one person who was responsible but it also made that person more of an advocate for achieving accreditation rather than resisting the process because it was complicated and too much work. We will have our official site visit from JCAH soon and will learn shortly thereafter if we will be accredited. The effort has been successful and gotten people involved.

Successes are much easier to recollect than failures, but both are critical to sound planning for the future. I would say that my successes as an administrator include first of all salvaging a very important organization which was on the brink of disaster. Second, I believe I have had an influence focusing attention on Indian alcoholism in the Pacific Northwest. Third, I have secured modern facilities for our inpatient alcohol/drug treatment program and a consolidated, newly-constructed home for all our outpatient services. Fourth, I pushed our organization to measure its quality against one of the most rigorous and rigid standards available, and became the first urban Indian clinic to receive JCAH accreditation. Finally, and most important, I have allowed myself to heal and grow within. This has improved my ability to lead and relate to other people more than anything.

Failures have occurred, as well. During the initial turmoil of my tenure at SIHB, I made some difficult decisions about cutbacks and dealing with other employees who appeared to be over their heads. I did not provide the listening time, sensitivity, and compassion to some of these people which they certainly deserved. Losing one's job is a tremendous stress. I still would like to relive that time so I could deal more humanely with staff layoffs. A second failure I see is the lack of proper attention I gave to building a strong board of directors. Clearly, there is some short-sighted self-interest behind this, but the success of an agency depends on the longevity of its community support.

PREPARATION AND LESSONS LEARNED

I am thirty-three years old and am a member of the Nez Perce Tribe of Idaho. My mother is full-blood Nez Perce, my father is German, and I am one of seven children who grew up in Seattle, Washington. There were some very rough times growing up—alcoholism in the home and a lot of poverty. During some good times, I was fortunate to spend periods with my grandparents who live on the reservation learning and talking about things that children need to hear but do not get when there is alcohol or domestic violence in the home. Too often, leaders in minority communities are reluctant to turn around and look at ourselves closely to see what destructive things are occurring within our homes and within our families. We should pay special attention to these areas so our children will have better opportunities and a better understanding of who they are rather than looking exclusively at the outside society as the source of the problem. That must change in order for us to achieve the things that we really want to achieve. Who we are is all a mixture of how we were raised and the influences that crossed our paths as we sought to get an education, to develop a career, to raise a family, and to live a meaningful life. Much of my upbringing centered around the good things, but in my family there were negative things as well. I think my experiences are fairly typical of many Indian families and possibly other populations from lower socioeconomic backgrounds. As minority administrators, we need to make sure we are honest with ourselves, that we seek to understand our past and how it affects our current attitudes and behavior.

I graduated from high school in 1971, and was fortunate to receive a variety of university scholarships available to minority students. I attended the University of Minnesota for the first three years of college. At my first counselling session with my adviser, I was informed that I had scored very highly in sciences and mathematics. In fact, I scored so high in math that I was "exempt" from taking any college math if I wanted to be exempt, and I could go ahead and take some other courses. I was seventeen and I thought, "Well, that's great! So I don't have to take any math." So I did not take any, and I went ahead and chose some other classes in liberal arts. It was not until after I graduated from college and wanted to get into the School of Public Health at the University of California at Berkeley that I realized how foolish it was for me to pass up the opportunity for college math. I was faced with a competitive group of fellow graduate students who had had college math, and we were all entering biostatistics. There was an assumption that you had a basic level of understanding of statistics, which was not true in my case. That was one lesson that I learned and that I try to pass on, especially when I talk to groups of high school students who might be going on to college. I tell them to take the math and hard sciences that might be available. I received my master's in public health in 1979. Throughout this period, I also spent a lot of time supplementing my income by working in a variety of different jobs, most of which related to health care or human services for Indian populations.

One of the reasons that I chose to go into the field of public health was the feeling that something needs to be done concerning the health care of Indian people. But I was not really sure how I could fit into that challenge. Many times I would attend funerals or hear of deaths of people who were very young, very talented, very gifted with intellectual or athletic ability. But they became a statistic that seems to plague Indian populations and other minority populations more severely than the general public. I knew that I did not want to become a medical doctor, because I could not stand the sight of blood or the thought of putting a needle into somebody, but I knew that I wanted to get involved in health care. The field of health care administration was an area that I fell into as a result of my efforts to get involved in health care programs in whatever way I could. I began writing grant applications, describing programs, and helping to plan programs for small nonprofit groups in the city of Minneapolis, for my home reservation in Idaho, and in the city of Seattle.

When I completed my program at the School of Public Health, I had a much better understanding of public health and how the health-care arena was constructed, or, more accurately, incrementally disjointed. The United States has one of the least responsive health care systems in the entire developed world. It is second only to South Africa in how it restricts health care to the marketplace, a privilege for only those who can afford to purchase care. It is really a capital industry, which is different than most of the industrialized nations throughout the world. Other developed nations have some form of national health insurance to assure that its populations are going to have health care regardless of income, race, or age. You really do not think about health care in the United States if you have an employer who provides insurance or has some way to take care of your health, but for Indian populations and other poverty populations, it is a real problem. It is a problem that is only recognized when people show up in ambulances and hospital emergency rooms without the resources to pay, or experience a medical catastrophe that totally depletes all their resources.

The U.S. health care arena is very disjointed. Those people who have health care coverage are pretty much provided for, and what is left are pockets of people—black people, Hispanic people, migrants, Indian people on reservations and Indian people in urban areas, the underemployed or working poor all referred to as "medically indigent." There is a system of nonprofit community-based organizations in the United States that attempts to address some of these health care needs with federal as well as private funding.

There are some positive and some negative things that I have learned as a minority administrator. It has been much easier for me as an Indian woman to convince people of the importance of this agency and the work that we are doing because it is genuinely important to me. If you need to pull in support and convince people, you need to be convinced yourself before you start talking to folks. In my organization a lot of times the reverse happens. Non-Indian employees often are very reluctant to deal with any personnel problems that might be associated with Indian employees, more so, I believe. It is a hands-off approach—I guess the non-Indian supervisor felt the response should be hands off of this Indian person because this is an Indian agency, my boss is Indian, and I am just going to have to figure out how to work around this person rather than dealing, like a good supervisor should, with whatever the personnel problem might be.

As a nonprofit agency, we need to devise a way to advance Indian people by providing outside training. At this point, it is a luxury we have not been able to afford to the degree that it makes a substantial impact on a person's income and advancement. We just cannot spend the money for someone to go to school and not to be in the clinic. That needs to change. Another issue that always arises is that people feel we do not employ enough Indians, even though our work force is 70 percent Indian. We do, however, need to recruit Indian physicians, dentists, CPAs, and other professionals.

It is very important for minority administrators to come into their positions, whether it is in local government or in the nonprofit sector, with a sense of competence, a desire for excellence, and a commitment to improve the services by participation and leadership. I agree wholeheartedly that if all we are doing is taking the place of a nonminority person without making those other changes, then we are really not fulfilling our responsibility. We have to break through and create a channel for other people to enter the system, so they can improve services which, I believe, is our ultimate goal: to elevate the health and well-being of the minority groups that we represent.

As a minority administrator, you will be asked to participate in a number of areas. For example, I am currently chairing the Mayor's Task Force for Downtown Human Services, which is a special task force that has just begun to respond to the rapid development and displacement of low-income housing and social services for low-income people. A city ordinance provides bonus incentives for downtown developers who want to build skyscrapers above a certain elevation. If they want to go above the elevation, they have to provide space for downtown human services, because many of the low-income housing and services and shelters and feeding programs for homeless people in the downtown areas are being eliminated by downtown development. So, in essence, if they want to expand their buildings over a certain elevation, they have to kick in for human-service space, provide funding to purchase space, or provide space for day-care centers.

I have also been very involved at the national level. Over the last four years, I have had to become a skilled lobbyist with the United States Congress. This has occurred primarily because 50 percent of our budget comes directly from congressional appropriations. Deliberations begin in January and, hopefully, a decision is made before October 1, although that has rarely been the case. These funds are crucial for the survival of our organization. I have the responsibility to keep people informed and to keep our staff informed about whether or not they are going to get a paycheck at the end of September. The Seattle congressional delegation has joined the fight in Washington, D.C., to save appropriations for Indian health. I think that we have made the northwest delegation from Washington, Oregon, and Alaska leaders in the Indian Health struggle nationally.

One of the other projects that might be of interest is a coalition with other Indian organizations. For many years, decision makers in Seattle local government waited for the Indian community to "get its act together" and, as in many minority communities, the internal struggles and the dirty laundry became a bigger agenda item than moving forward. Over the past three years, I have been very involved in working with other Indian organizations to establish our peace plan and to work cooperatively toward a single objective. That has been a major accomplishment and one that has enabled us to become much more effective in dealing with the city of Seattle in 1988. The fruits of this labor will result in newly constructed space to centralize services for the Indian population in the Seattle area, to be called "The Leschi Center."

Sometimes people feel that it is acceptable for programs operated on behalf of the poor and minorities to use lower standards. I am working to show that the Seattle Indian Health Board is a competently run, financially sound, and top-quality service agency; and that low-income people deserve just as rigid a standard for quality care as anybody else, including those with the cash to pay for services. I am trying to convince other providers of low-income health care to do the same and to set tough standards for ourselves and to live up to them. Minority administrators should never do any less!

I think my strength is the ability to communicate with people on an individual level, which is important for any administrator. Once you lose your ability to communicate, you begin making decisions in isolation. No matter how good you are, that is a formula for failure, for loss of support, and for loss of good decision making.

Over time, I have changed my view of management, my own self-perception as the director of an agency encountering various crises. When I first started, I admit that I had an extreme amount of paranoia and have regretted my views. I was suspicious of those people who might want to help, and I tried to determine how they would benefit by our demise. I would always use a formula when I met someone: "Let me see, now are they on my side or their side?" I could never really be sure. It was not a happy time and, as a result, I have changed my style considerably. Peace of mind has come by accepting that I am not responsible for everything that is going to happen and every decision does not have to be my decision. There are a lot of good people out there who want to help; do not burn any bridges so they will come back.

One of my strengths is a willingness to try to surround myself with people who know more than I do about what it is that we are doing. I like to have good legal advice, good accounting and financial advice, good advice from folks involved in whatever a particular decision might be. That is very important and is not something that I have always done. This approach is one that has evolved over time. I see a big difference in how I make decisions now and how I made decisions when I first took this job when I was really suspicious of everybody. I just cannot emphasize enough the value of getting as good advice as you can without delaying the decision-making process. You should develop your own little network of people to bounce ideas off, regardless of the substantive areas. You also need political advice on what the downside of a decision may be.

One of my weaknesses is that in my current position, I have not paid enough attention to creating an incentive for people to get training, to further their education and advance, whether it is within this organization or to advance on to some other agency, thereby growing and representing our community better. That is one area that I know I need to make a priority. I am sure I could convince some big corporations to give us a scholarship for one or two outstanding employees a year. There are employees in my group who would be prime candidates for that type of incentive and award.

Programs like the School of Public Affairs here at Arizona State University are very important. Agencies ought to be looking toward providing trainee incentives for people in the entry level or above to receive additional education and training. Minority administrators should explore all good training opportunities. Some corporations even provide free assistance as a part of their community relations programs. IBM has a very big management training institute that gives scholarships for minority communities, and, I think, in nonprofit settings. You need to make it a priority.

COMMUNITY RELATIONSHIPS

As I said earlier, I think support systems are important. But by definition, you have to feel good about a support system and choose its members judiciously. A good deal of my support comes from these networks. I would recommend that you use your network of colleagues in similar organizations and other contacts or political acquaintances that you might have. It is also important to have personal support systems, e.g., a spouse, good friends, or family. They round out your perspective of the world. For a long time, when I first started on this job, my assistant at work was also a friend that I saw on weekends, that I talked to on the telephone. It was just twenty-four hours of nothing but what was happening at the Seattle Indian Health Board. That is not healthy. You need to balance out your life. You need to deal with your unit or your department, but you also must know what is happening nationally with similar organizations and you should have some contacts in that group, some network dealing with local politics, and some handle on how you are doing yourself emotionally. Self-development and a good self-perception are very important, too.

There is a very active minority community in the city of Seattle, and minority-focused agencies have formed a group called the Minority Executive Directors' Coalition, which is patterned after United Way. The Minority Executive Directors' Coalition meets monthly to talk about a variety of things of mutual interest, and that has been a real interesting experience. There have been some real positive outcomes, as well as some bitter fights. There is always going to be that political element whenever you get people together to organize formally in order to leverage power. Basically, whoever calls the shots is the force that keeps things moving during the meetings.

At one time in Walla Walla prison, the Hispanic inmates and the Indian inmates were fighting, and there were a couple of people killed. As a result, the leadership from the Indian community and the Hispanic community in Seattle communicated through the State of Washington Department of Corrections that "We want to go in there and get people together." This coalition started going out to the prisons, meeting as a group, and basically getting the Indian and Hispanic people to talk to the inmates and to say, "This is crazy. Knock it off. We have got a lot of similarities and a lot of reasons to try to work together." Consequently, we have some very constructive things occurring in the prison. This is a good example of how minority communities can work together.

Within my agency, the issue of minority employees really has not come up. If there is ever any friction about employment, it is centered around Indian employees: Is this going to be an Indian employee or a non-Indian employee? That seems to be the gauge that people use. We do have a few black, Asian, and Hispanic employees. Maybe people figure this is an Indian agency. But the issue of other minority groups in employment practices has not come up as a problem.

I am currently the president of the Minority Executive Directors Coalition (MEDC) of King County, a fifty-member network which meets monthly to share common information and support each other. We have gone to the mat with local government on issues affecting minorities. It has happened that on one occasion I alienated staff in the mayor's office on issues of minorities, when these same people were supportive and friendly on issues of Indian health. The MEDC forum allows most potentially explosive issues between minority groups to be nipped in the bud.

I do not serve as spokesperson for minority interests. I have a rule of thumb that I follow: I do not speak for minority communities. I often speak at events sponsored by minority communities, and they will have a lot of different people there who ask, "Will you come on behalf of the Indian community?" And I will say, "Well, okay, I will come and give my point of view, but I cannot really say that I am speaking for the Indian community without being fairly presumptuous." I try to preface my remarks with, "I am giving my perspective as an Indian woman. It might not be the same as another Indian woman's perspective, and it sure might not be the same as a black or Hispanic male or female." So as far as speaking for the minority community, I do not think I have ever really done that. I do not think I would unless there was some sort of process where one has input from all the different minority groups and that input was gathered into one place and it could be said, "Okay, here is the position that everybody agrees to. Will you read it?" I would say, "Okay."

I have served on selection panels for the mayor's office to fill one of the mayor's department-head positions, and I have pulled together a selection panel. When I have the responsibility to put a panel together, I try to get as eclectic a group as possible. I pull together an Indian, a black, a Hispanic, an Asian, and whites from women's groups or businesses or downtown development. When I am invited to serve on a selection panel, I always feel uncomfortable because I know that I am there because I am Indian. But then, on the other hand, I want to be there because it is a real good opportunity to screen people, and try to influence the process so that minorities have access to positions.

On the opposite side of the coin is the responsibility to see that minorities are not interviewed for appearances. I was in a situation where a minority person was being pushed as a finalist, but everybody agreed that the person could not do the job. I spoke against putting that person in the final three because I do not think we are doing our minority people any favors by trying to promote somebody into a position of responsibility who clearly is not competent to handle it. Well, the mayor had three people, he made his choice, and he did not pick this minority person. But we all agreed that this was not the best person and this person could not do the job. That was a situation where I had a difference of opinion with some other minority people who were also on the panel. I think that the best service we can do for communities is to have competent minority people in positions of authority. The worst thing we could do is to try to push incompetent minority people, because that will make it even twice as bad for competent minority people.

GOALS FOR THE MINORITY COMMUNITY

The major goal I have for the minority community is to see minority populations given the respect they deserve from local government to analyze and solve their problems from within. Too often, local government wants to solve "neighborhood" problems but does not want to touch "population" problems. The result of this approach is a constantly migrating problem within specific populations, such as homicide, youth suicide, alcoholism, and homelessness. When the neighborhood tires of the problem, it migrates elsewhere and the neighborhood suddenly becomes more white. Population-based planning and service delivery is needed to begin empowering minorities to develop their own communities.

UNIQUE PROBLEMS/OPPORTUNITIES DUE TO MINORITY STATUS

Sometimes it is frustrating dealing as a representative of the Indian community because in Seattle we do make up less than 1 percent of the population. Right now I am working with the other Indian agencies in Seattle to try to develop a new facility for our services at the Indian Center to provide senior housing. We are running into opposition from the neighborhood we want to move into. How big a vote we represent to the city, the city council, and to the mayor's office has come into play. Usual allies are now leaning toward this neighborhood that might represent a much larger vote in city elections. It has been disheartening, but it is a challenge as well.

Being a minority administrator, you realize that there are prejudices among some people in decision-making positions. However, I do not think it is really overwhelming. I think that a lot of it depends on how you personally come across and talk with people and deal with people. In my current position, for sure, it is an advantage to be Indian, and I think it has been an advantage to be a woman. It is my theory that a lot of the health problems experienced by Indian people can be addressed by dealing with and targeting women, because many of the decisions about family health care, child health care, and prenatal care are made by women—who usually bring the kids in. We are not doing enough for women, which is another factor in domestic violence and in alcoholism treatment. Those services just have not been available.

In dealing in a larger bureaucracy like city government or state government, there would be some real obstacles as a minority woman. In fact, I think the obstacles are even greater for a woman than for a minority in terms of positions of authority and decision making. Again, I think there are more stereotypes about women not being able to make decisions or becoming emotional or not willing to have a confrontation, or to play hardball. Male minority administrators might experience racial prejudices, but I think for minority women it is really doubly difficult in positions of administrative responsibility.

6

Tucson: Changing the Complexion of City Government

Joel Valdez

INTRODUCTION

Tucson is a charter city and has operated since 1929 under the council-manager form of government. Those familiar with this form of government will understand that the charter, like the Constitution of Arizona or the Constitution of the United States, sets forth certain powers, duties, and responsibilities for line officers, the city manager, the mayor, and the council. It is modelled after a corporate structure similar to the way that IBM or other large corporations are operated, with the electorate as the stockholders and the mayor and council as the board of directors. The mayor is chairman of the board and the manager is the president of the corporation.

The charter grants certain powers to city officials. For instance, in Tucson, the mayor and council may only appoint the city manager, city clerk, city attorney, and the magistrates. The primary power to make other appointments is vested in the city manager. One exception is that the personnel director is appointed and removed by the Civil Service Commission, which itself is appointed by the mayor and council for five-year overlapping terms. This procedure was developed primarily to prevent politicizing the civil services. The personnel director does not report to me but works very closely with me, because in our system of checks and balances, he cannot spend money without the city manager's approval.

As city manager, I serve at the pleasure of the mayor and council. Any time four council members wish to remove me, they can do so by simply telling me to clean out my desk. There is no tenure, contract, or security in this position. I also do not have an employment agreement; it is prohibited. So, for thirteen years I have lived on the edge, but I like the job. I am a native Tucsonian. I grew up in the barrios and went to school in the city. I know the city, and more importantly, I know my enemies. City councils come and go, and the managers are usually the ones who have to go first when the council changes. This has not happened in Tucson for thirteen years. The mayor has been there through four terms. My council has been reelected, four of them three times and three of them two times. So there is continuity, which makes a difference.

Since 1976, Tucson has basically had the same people serving in office. This kind of continuity helps in the administrative area because we have individuals who understand how the city works and who is really supposed to do what for whom. It has made my job a lot easier. Since my appointment in April 1974, I have appointed all of the department heads with the exception of one. I inherited the finance director. He will retire this July, and I will promote a woman who will become the first female finance director of a large city in the United States.

BUDGET

Cities, like private businesses, need to show a "profit" at the end of the fiscal year. The "profit" is in the form of a carry-forward which is very important. If, at the end of the year, you had $9 million carry-forward, you have made a profit, but if you did not have any carry-forward on June 30, you cannot pay your bills in July. With our spending limit laws in Arizona, for various reasons we have never spent the full amount that we budgeted. We have a combined budget approach—the capital budget and the operating budget—which totalled $308 million in fiscal year 1986. The budget tells the public every penny we propose to spend from every source.

I have never spent the full budget. In the capital component—about $100 million—there are not enough contractors in the state to produce everything you say you are going to do. We know automatically that we are going to have a carry-forward in that area, but it is restricted funding. However, in the operating budget, we have funds for 600 policemen, and about the best we can do is 575; the remaining money for the other 25 is automatically going to carry-forward. We still produce a satisfactory level of police services, but it is with 575 as opposed to 600 officers. As city administrators, we have a responsibility to produce optimum service at the least possible cost.

PERSONNEL

We saw Gramm-Rudman-Hollings coming about three years ago, so I have been salting away money at least to replace the loss of revenue sharing. I was one of the members of a national committee to revive revenue sharing in 1981, but at that time, the White House and Congress were telling us it was going to die next time. So I asked the council, "If you lose $7.5 million overnight, how are you going to make it up? You can increase property tax but that's 2 percent a year. You can get another penny on the sales tax, if the people vote for it. What are you going to do?" They said, like Will Rogers, "That's what we pay you for." I said, "Okay, that's all I want to hear." So, I started squirrelling money away and when we went into the next fiscal year $7.5 million short, I had already replaced that with monies that we had set aside. That was not easy, because city employees wanted a 7 percent raise. We only granted 4 percent and squirrelled away 3 percent. As a result, we will be going into the next year in very good shape.

In 1974 when I was appointed, there were 4,439 employees as compared to 4,100 today. Yet, our population is up 60,000 people and the area we service has grown by roughly thirty square miles. Flexibility in personnel has allowed us to increase service delivery while decreasing the number of city employees. The philosophy is to allot money into capital equipment and cut back on the bodies. For instance, a gang mower does not draw a pension but eliminates three personnel slots. Conversion of the garbage system from three-men crews to two to one-man crews saves money. Yet the human element is always taken into account. We always have to have more workers in the streets division for the overlay program, spring-fall, but instead of laying people off, we move them from sanitation into the streets division. They are needed in that division because when you are tossing cans and a man gets to be fifty-five, back problems develop. We move them to less strenuous work.

About ten years ago, we did some personnel planning concerning when individuals would retire and the distribution of personnel. This allows me to move people around easily. I can take the fifty-five–year-olds and put them on the one-man trucks and put the younger ones back out on the other trucks tossing cans. With the increased flexibility of being able to freeze ten slots here and add them over there, or taking the money for those ten and using it somewhere else, we have increased productivity with less cost. Our property tax in 1974 was $1.75 per $100; today, it is $0.68. We put through a $330 million bond program in 1984 which will raise the property tax to about $1.00. But it will still be less than the 1974 rate.

ADMINISTRATIVE PHILOSOPHY

There are certain rules of thumb that city managers are taught from day one. First, never surprise your council. Councils should not read in the newspaper that you have been working on something they have not been informed of. That is lesson number one. By the same token, if you do not inform the council, then do not get upset if the council pulls surprises on you. The most emphatic word I can use is *trust*. If I trust you, then we can argue like hell and then go have a beer. But if I do not trust you, we argue and fight and do not resolve anything. So when I have a dispute with a councilman, I go have a beer with him and ask, "What's bugging you?" and "What's your problem?" All of a sudden you have turned the tables. You have done a 180 degree turn and most of the time it was something small, such as he did not get the message about what was going on. His aide did not tell him, or he did not get the message, and a reporter called him at home and caught him off guard.

I have found over the years that probably the most deadly irritant to an elected official is to be made to look ignorant, that he did not know. If they know that it was not my fault, they will apologize afterward. But, at that instant at ten o'clock at night, when the reporter was yelling at him or questioning him about something that he should have known about, then it is normal that he gets mad. And I say, "It was on your desk. I know because your secretary put it there. I told you, but you didn't read it." They find it on their desk and they owe me an apology. But the key word is *trust*. When I work with my department heads, it is on the same basis. I delegate a lot of authority to my department heads. You hire the best person possible and let him do the job. If I hire you and have to tell you every day what to do, then I made a mistake. I do not have that kind of time. Therefore, the trust that the city council gives to me, I transfer on to the department heads.

My relationship with my department heads is very personal—one on one. I take a personal interest in how they run their departments and treat the people within them. I have picked up garbage. I have been in the sewer lines. I have been out with the asphalt crews in the summertime. I wanted to know what it is like to pick up garbage in 120 degrees, so when the garbagemen are complaining, at least I have an idea of what they are talking about. All too often department heads who have never experienced the conditions under which people work have a hard time understanding when the employee complains. So I have found it very useful to go out in the field. I know what they go through. I have swept floors, ridden in police cars and on fire engines, and have been in the helicopter. However, it is also an opportunity for meeting the troops. Some supervisors say they have lunch with the managers. Well, I have lunch with my garbage guys. They always go to a certain restaurant so I will go there and sit with them. I do the same thing with the fire fighters and the police, it does not matter.

I start my day early. In the summertime, I start about 6:00 A.M., setting sessions up at 6:30 and breakfast is at 7:00. I used to deliver newspapers and worked all night, so I have an automatic alarm clock. Five o'clock I am up. So, rather than sit around and do nothing, I will go hit the crews. The garbage guys start at 5:30, or 5:00 in the summertime, and I know they always have menudo, so I head for headquarters. The same with fire station 1. They always have menudo on the stove. It is my philosophy—treat people like human beings and they will treat you like a human being.

The people I hire for command positions are academically prepared—they have credentials. But they also have had some lessons from the "school of hard knocks." If someone has had some part-time jobs and worked his or her way through school, that person has a little edge above the person who has never worked, just attended school. Because we are in the public service, we have to know how to take the heat. You never can fully satisfy the public who is paying the bills. You would be surprised at the number of people I interview who cannot take the very first pressured confrontation with an irate citizen. Well, I cannot have those individuals on my staff. So I am looking for individuals who are mature, know what it is to go hungry, and have been there before. I think it gives you a little different outlook when you are at this upper level, having to deal with the haves and the have-nots we are trying to serve. There is something there that you must develop that you are never going to learn from books. No school is going to teach that. Individuals who have come through those programs—internships, the National Urban Fellows, and other university internships—will be better prepared to handle pressurized situations.

Policy making in administrative areas is pretty much left to me. Public policy is a different matter. I assist the mayor and council in the formulation and implementation of public policy but seldom "create" public policy alone. Administrative policy also is a different issue. Some managers create and implement administrative policy without input from others. I prefer to utilize a participatory management style and involve the affected parties through committee structures to draft proposed policy. For some administrative policy, I obtain mayor and council approval. Those are basically issues involving funding. Other areas, such as work schedules, time off, use of sick leave, grievance procedures, etc., are created/modified through the participatory process.

INNOVATIONS AND SUCCESSES

I have created flexibility within the budget system with the understanding of the city council. I first draft a budget and submit it to the council. After the council's adoption, it is my budget and my orders are to implement it. Since I have $220 million to administer the city and I can do it for less, there is no problem. They are not going to get on my case. But, if I go over $220 million, then I am in trouble. Within that framework there is an understanding that if they grant me thirty more policemen on July 1, specifically for five sergeants, a couple of lieutenants and so forth, after July 1 the money is for thirty slots. After July 1, if the chief says, "No, I am only going to put on four sergeants and one lieutenant, because I want more field guys," I have the full authority to do that, as long as I stay within that thirty. If I go above the thirty, then I must go back to the council and seek concurrence. I have to have that flexibility. Otherwise, a manager cannot function.

You would be surprised how many organizations are still performing functions that are no longer needed, but they are doing it "because we've always done it that way." I say, "Haven't you ever thought about getting rid of it?" To this end, I created a team called the "Resource Management Group" which is located in the budget office. This group consists of an economist, a time-motion person, and other related individuals. A department head might complain, "Oh, man, we've got to have this secretarial position, we're really hurting." What do I know? I do not work there, but I will grant it if the council okays it. Ninety days later, this team goes in to see what the person in the new position is doing. If the person is not doing anything and it is clear the unit does not need the position, the person is transferred to another unit where a real need has been identified. As long as it is the same position—clerk typist I or secretary I—they can laterally transfer people to any function in the city. Thus, except in fire and police, the department head who comes in and really makes a case for a certain kind of position can expect to have an internal audit through this team sometime within ninety days.

We have also moved heavily into computerization. I got fascinated with the computer and learned at night. All of a sudden four or five department heads had to have computers. I told them way in advance that we were going to computerize. I sent some to school—provided the same opportunity to everybody—and when it came down to compensation review, those who got the training got a 7 percent raise; those who did not got zero. They were not too happy. They are now heavily into training. I have a modem in my house, and I receive messages at night. Some of my department heads are at the office at night, and the computers greatly improve our administrative capabilities.

I still have one fellow who just is deathly afraid of the machine, like he is going to break it or something. He just cannot use it, so he is still sending me written memos. I send responses back on the tube. He will call my secretary and say that he hasn't received an answer. My secretary will say, "He sent it. It's on the tube. Log on." He has his secretary log on and then we find out, so we change his code word. I am bound and determined that this fellow is going to use the tube. I do not care if communications are misspelled, I am just going to get him onto it. Why? Because he is a commander and a tough department head. He has 1,100 or 1,200 employees but he just will not get with it. Yet his division commanders, his deputies, and his section heads are all on the tube. So you are going to be chasing after your staff saying, "Wait for me, I'm your leader." They left you a year ago. How are you going to communicate with them? He will say, "Well, I've got a secretary! She's got a tube." "You can't do that!" "Oh, yes I can." I will make a convert out of him. He is going to find out it is fun. You become a slave to the damned thing, but nevertheless that is the wave of the future, and if you do not learn to use it, how can I expect my other department heads to do it?

My major successes as a city manager include improvements in debt management, a volunteer program that has grown to 800 participants, significant annexations to protect the financial integrity and future of the city, and considerable progress implementing affirmative action both in municipal employment and in city contracts. Each of these successes came in a different area and, of course, there were different participants, issues, obstacles, and approaches. However, one strategy that I used in all of these was close cooperation with both the mayor and city council, as well as considerable reliance on strong staff members.

My chief failure was the inability to obtain approval of a major transportation street plan that involved five jurisdictions. Both in my city and elsewhere, among the most difficult problems are those which require interjurisdictional solutions. Political, economic, and other differences frequently make it complex to solve regional problems—whether they are in transportation, as in this case, or concern the environment, water, etc.

Probably my greatest weakness is the inability to terminate someone who is just about average. They may really be trying, but they just cannot hack it. And yet, my job is to get rid of them. Well, I will go to great lengths to try to find something else for them to do rather than throw them out, especially if they have a family. That is probably my greatest weakness and I admit it; I have a problem. But if the person is corrupt, I have no problem sending them to prison. I do not care who they are. Even relatives. I did not realize it, but I had fired my wife's cousin who was on the police force. I did not know, but I fired him for ticket fixing. Well, several members of the family do not talk to me. That is too bad.

PREPARATION AND LESSONS LEARNED

When I was with the juvenile court in 1966, I had climbed as high as I could. I was number two in command and the individual there was young and there was no chance of me ever doing anything other than being number two. Mark Keane, city manager of Tucson in 1966, had created a mid-management program with an eye toward creating some future city managers. He called. I had met him because I served once as a traffic referee and I happened to have his son before me, not serious stuff, so we struck up a friendship. When he created the program, he called and said, "I know it's a pay cut, but there is a potential here for you if you want to take it." So I went home one afternoon and told my wife I had quit. She said, "You what?" I said, "Yes, we are going to take off on a different track." That is how I got into the city business.

In the juvenile court I was basically doing all the day-to-day administration of a court system with a staff of about 120 and a $10 million budget. Mark Keane wanted me to go to the city and do the same thing for all the library systems. There were fourteen branches, a regional/city/county system, and since I worked for the county I knew the county policies. I built the first bilingual branch in the western United States, which was copied by Albuquerque. Again, I understood what people were telling me from the barrios, "We sure would like to have some books in Spanish." The only Spanish-language theater in Tucson was levelled by urban renewal. So I introduced, again paying attention to the folks, Mexican films. I brought them in from Los Angeles. We could not show them enough and did not have space. They took off like wildfire to the degree that the private sector saw that there was profit to be made and then they opened a Spanish-language theater again. I did the same with the theater needs in the black community.

It is unique for a manager to be a manager of his own city. But it sure helps when you have grown up in the world of "have-nots" to understand and never forget. I know my grandparents and relatives say, "Just because you are up here, someday you may be back down here. Never forget." So I do a lot of managing by wandering around. I have no problem in the barrios and I will talk about administrative issues, baptisms, or whatever. It does not matter. I am all over the city.

After I agreed in May 1966 to go to the city, the city manager was fired in August. I had already closed the door behind me and I said, "Well, the Lord has got to open a window there somewhere." It was open, but I did not know if he was still going to keep me. So I went to the then acting manager—Mr. O'Mara—and he assigned me to the libraries as promised. It was supposed to be a six-month turnover of rotating assignments, but I was there from 1966 to 1969 or 1970, because the acting manager, who became permanent, did away with the program. Those of us who were still there were stuck in the departments. I then moved into the city manager's office as an administrative assistant. I just happened to be at the right place at the wrong time when they hired a new manager in December 1972 (after O'Mara) and then fired him in December 1973. I had been doing all the work. Some of the council said, "Why don't you apply?" and I said, "What are my chances?" "Pretty good, maybe." The worst they could do is say no, and we were used to that. So when they said yes and did it, then I said, "Well, I got it and I can't drop it." I just did the best I could, and I stayed with it. It is not the easiest job in the world, let me tell you. But, it is very rewarding public service, if you really know that you are there to provide a service.

The primary factors promoting success can be employed by both minority and nonminority administrators. The key is to set your sights on a goal and to work diligently toward it. You will face setbacks, we all do, but don't give up and don't lose sight of your goals. Internal fortitude is an important dimension of successful people. Don't quit on yourself. Be honest with yourself and with others; honesty will come back to reward you. If you know you're weak in a given area, admit it and get assistance. Surround yourself with good and candid people, and don't be afraid to surround yourself with talented people who might be smarter than you.

Additional and continual training is a key. I send two people to Harvard every year, particularly those individuals I believe have the potential to be department heads five years from now. We have advanced degree work at 100 percent cost of tuition reimbursement at universities. I also send people to the University of Michigan, Wharton, Stanford, and UCLA. We are dickering with the FBI academy on some new program they want to try. The police will go there and also to Northwestern University.

In light of the future direction of public administration, if an individual is a freshman at the university and starting out in a public administration program, the first thing I will ask them is, "Can you use a computer?" "Well, no I haven't..." I say, "You better get with it, because the employees you are going to hire are going to leave you behind. You are not going to be able to talk the same language." The importance of this skill is being brought home to many managers today. For example, I am working with a group of the administrators who got into the public service business, particularly cities, during the era of a lot of federal aid a decade ago. Their only experience in managing a city is with a tremendous amount of federal aid; therefore they do not know how to manage without as much money. These are managers who just became managers, say, in the last ten years. They are in their late thirties, mid-forties, and concerned if they will survive. Can they survive? How do you go to your city council and tell them you are losing $10 million, you have got to raise property taxes or you have got to do this, or you have got to lay off. We really have never had to do that until now. Computers are an essential tool to help one make crucial choices between services to continue and services to curtail. Consequently, computer literacy is a must for minority administrators. On a personal note I continue to seek out seminars on various subjects which will enhance my knowledge. I believe one does not stop learning until one dies. In 1972 I was given an opportunity by then city manager, Roger O'Mara, to attend the MIT Sloan School of Management. This intense course convinced me that I could compete with the best and do all right. I returned with a conviction that my ethnicity was an asset, not a liability. In 1974 I was appointed city manager.

In 1978 President Carter selected me for the White House Conference on Balanced National Growth and Economic Development. This came out of the blue and I accepted. In May 1978 he asked if I wanted to attend the Senior Managers in Government Program at Harvard. This program is for federal senior managers only, so this also came as a surprise. The mayor and council OK'd my leave and I received some of the best education today on administering a public agency. The point I want to make is take advantage of educational opportunity whenever it comes your way.

COMMUNITY RELATIONSHIPS

Affiliation with the formal and informal power structure of a cross section of the community is a must. I am a member of Tucson Rotary, the largest rotary club in Tucson, which contains a majority of the influential members of the community. My affiliation with the University of Arizona and Pima Community College also affords me weekly contacts with a cross section of our community.

The minority community presents a different problem since there is not a single recognized organization such as Rotary. However, participating in Hispanic activities is a cultural must, since I am Hispanic. In addition, I have enjoyed the activities of the black, Jewish, Greek, Italian, Oriental, and Native American communities and am always welcomed to attend their social and cultural events. Being a part of the total community is one of the great satisfactions of this job.

Tucson is almost 30 percent Hispanic, 3 percent black, 1 percent Native American, and the rest white. My position when I received it was unique in that there have been Hispanic assistant managers for at least twenty years in Tucson, but never managers. With that high a preponderance of Hispanic population, one has to ask, "How come?" And it may be that one of the problems that minority administrators have is that once one is there, the majority of society automatically assumes that the only persons hired will be of that ethnic background, which is not true. It is just not true, but there is an assumption and a perception which is difficult to deal with. The lament of the public servant is that no matter what you do, you are either right or wrong. You are damned if you do and damned if you don't. If I hire a Hispanic, they say, "What do you expect, he is Hispanic." All right, if I do not hire the Hispanic, then the Hispanic community says, "You sold out." You cannot win, no matter what you do. But I hope that the person I have selected is very conscious about affirmative action goals and what we are trying to do.

We have been grooming a young woman to become finance director for about three and one-half years. And rather than go through the motions, it is much better to be up front with people, candidates, and say, "We are going to recruit in-house; we are not going to go outside." If we are going to go outside, then that truthfully means there is nobody in-house. If you have been developing someone in-house, then it is not fair to go through the motions of a national search only to disappoint a lot of people. So this person has been pegged already for three and one-half years of grooming. I am committed to affirmative action and have developed the plan. Since there are no female finance directors in the United States, how can I bring one in? I must train from within.

I already have the concurrence of the council, although we have made no announcement yet. To some it may sound unfair, but to those who have been left out all these years it is pretty fair. Anyway, there are some positions that require council concurrence, including public safety, fire and police, finance, purchasing, and, for some strange reason, the parks director.

Females have been underrepresented in command positions. We now have the library director and people will say that is traditionally female. It is not! Not a director of a total system. The one I brought in was director of the state library of Oregon. She now commands the city/county library system in Pima County. Most directors are males. Now, the assistant director of my transportation department will probably become the head of the department. All the male engineers look up to this lady who really knows her stuff. She has a Ph.D. in engineering.

I will have three females, two blacks, four Hispanics, and five Anglo white department heads after September. In 1974 we had all white commanders. So I set out to make changes in 1974 and got the council to approve. In fact, the day I was appointed city manager is the day they approved the affirmative action plan—two hours before. I was appointed by a four-to-three vote, not too strong, but I was there and set out then in my own mind to change the complexion of the city. With two females coming on board, I think I have done what I have set out to do.

I think one of my responsibilities is to identify minority people, to get them into the mainstream and start developing them professionally. I have served on oral boards for high-level positions in other cities, and there were no blacks or Hispanics who we interviewed. I do not know why, but they were not there. Under many civil service systems, including Tucson, supervisors can only pick from the list that is given to them. So we have a responsibility to make sure they get on those lists. That is why I say I am constantly developing people to make sure they at least get on a list. This way people cannot say there are no qualified candidates, because there are. But if they are not on the lists, then you have to bite the bullet. Instead of a rule of one in three you expand it to one in seven. My toughest area was in public safety. I finally broke the pattern and now you see a sprinkling of Hispanics and black commanders and females in the police department. That change was tough to bring about, but you have to be willing to stick your neck out.

When I was appointed assistant city manager in Tucson by O'Mara, I did not know the kind of pressure he had come under for appointing me. When he left he gave me a box of hate mail which said that he was ruining the city and he had just set the city back one hundred years, and so forth. You have to take chances. I cannot run the personnel department, but I sure have a lot of influence with the commissioners. I have to do the appointing from the lists that are given to me, but if those oral boards are all lily-white, I will never appoint from that list.

The personnel director is under mandate by the Civil Service Commission that the complexion of the oral board must reflect that of the community. So we do not have oral boards that are all of one race or one gender. They must be balanced. Some individuals are really difficult to find, e.g., a professional Native American, but we will fly them in if necessary. We use an Apache attorney, Ned Andersen, to help us out at times. That is how I broke the long tradition of the hiring practices of police departments. We have a new chief who is Hispanic—Ronstadt. I hired him. The other one retired and would never bite the bullet on hiring minorities. We made what we call a whole list of certification available to him and everyone who was qualified for the position. All you have to do is look at Spanish surnames, and there were ten of them on the list. But the union was so strong that you were required to pick number one.

For years the only ones who were up at the top of the list were all Jones and Smith. You could not reach the blacks and the Hispanics and many of the females because that list was old and out of date. I scrapped the list. They fought me and took me to court. The union said I tried to kill the list. The Arizona Civil Rights Commission said to scrap the list because the mix was not good. The union wanted to keep the list and filed an injunction. The court held it up for seven months, but finally we killed the list. Then they had a rule of one in three. When you have five positions you get fifteen names, and I knew that the first hundred names were all Jones and Smith, so I demanded a rule of one in seven. And then whole lists. Otherwise, we did not hire anyone.

TUCSON

And I had the council backing me up. If the council had not backed me up, then I would have been in trouble. That was the difference.

I don't allow myself to "speak" for the Hispanics in Tucson. There are plenty of leaders here. But I do serve on state, regional, and national committees to do what I can for Hispanics. There are times when I do work behind the scenes to assist someone in another jurisdiction who is being considered for a position or is being treated unfairly. I'm careful in this area but will act when asked.

GOALS FOR THE MINORITY COMMUNITY

I'd like to see people of all races in decision-making positions. It may be utopian, but if we don't try, it can never happen. I know I've had more successes than failures in this effort, and there have been successes in other cities, as well. In Tucson, I created an effort to bring together all races through cultural events and art programs. "Tucson Meet Yourself" is attended by over 20,000 people each year and is a sight to behold. All this because I wanted people of all walks of life to see that for at least one four-day weekend, they could peacefully exist. Another event, "The International Mariachi Conference," is now attracting thousands to our convention center for another multicultural, people-mixing event, not to mention the preservation of Mariachi music and all it portrays of the Hispanic culture.

From these activities comes the notion that minorities can produce, if the stereotypical images can be changed. Violence is not one of the approaches best suited to changing stereotypical images. Even gains from protest politics tend to be short-lived. To best change any system one should first get into the system and then influence decision making so that permanent change may follow. Equal opportunity for education, training and jobs, and a system to assure these equal opportunities, are essential.

UNIQUE PROBLEMS/OPPORTUNITIES DUE TO MINORITY STATUS

I don't seem to have too great a difficulty in Tucson. If the mayor and council are wrestling with an issue that has as its root cause "racism," I am able to sense it quicker than they, then work with many of the coalitions I've built to help us resolve it.

I have a great deal of influence over the personnel selection process. The system I set up states that people cannot be hired unless the Affirmative Action documentation has been provided. If the Affirmative Action officers, two blacks, two Hispanic, in their mind have questions about the hiring process and outcomes, their orders are to change things. Supervisors have got to justify why they picked a particular individual. I do not want to hear: "Because he's number one." They know the situation, so the department head has delegated this to the division head who has delegated this to the section head, and it is the section head who is going to make the selection and pass it back up the chain. That does not mean anything! Affirmative Action will block the hire. It will come directly to me, and they are all going to come and explain to me why. They do not like to do that. You can call it intimidation if you want, but if we mean what we say, then we have to enforce it. Every now and then one may slip by, but we have had a lot of success. We have been successful in changing the complexion of the city and we are not afraid to block an appointment.

The same situation exists for the termination of an employeee. If the person says, "I'm being terminated because I'm black, or Indian, or Hispanic," that rings bells, because I am the one who has to take the witness stand. I am the one they subpoena. I do not like to do that. Therefore, I take special care to see that this does not occur. Every now and then, we foul up, and I will reverse the termination order. I will grant full back pay and the person who was responsible may not like it, but they are now on ninety days probation. In a couple of cases, the person they tried to get rid of is now their boss. That is an interesting human relations problem.

Clearly, most of my influence is in non–civil service positions. I could hire off the street if I wanted to. I also give individuals in civil service positions the opportunity to be promoted to exempted positions. How you do that is by providing equal opportunities to receive training to everybody. If you have five deputy chiefs in the fire department, and you are already pretty sure that two or three have potential of being chiefs, you offer an educational opportunity to develop that potential. We are going to make training available to those who think they want to be chief in the future, and this may mean two weeks away from your family. You would be surprised, some of them say, "I don't want it. I don't want to be chief." Fine. Sign here that you do not want to take the training, that you have declined. We are offering training in computers on the clock, off the clock. You give an hour, we pay you an hour. "I'm not going to do that." Fine, sign here. You document their refusal. Comes time for some promotions, and I can either noncompetitively promote, without exam, or I can promote through the exam process. The system is flexible. If I go noncompetitive, they pull the files of the eligible people and if you have taken advantage of every opportunity that was there, and the person next to you was complaining about not being selected and never once made any effort, no court is going to overturn my appointment. You make the training available to everybody. You would be surprised how many secretaries do not want training in word processing. "I don't want to learn that stuff." Fine, use your IBM, but Susie over here is taking classes and in about six months we are going to have two positions that pay $300 more, but you are not going to be ready for it because we will noncompetitively promote. The best of those who took the training will get the promotions. Those who did not cannot say "I wasn't given the chance."

7

The New Sleuth: Administration in the Birthplace of the Old Confederacy

Reuben M. Greenberg

INTRODUCTION

My name is Reuben Greenberg, and I have been chief of police of Charleston, South Carolina, since 1982. Charleston is a city of 85,000 people, and we have the largest police department in the state—250 officers and 102 civilians. Prior to becoming chief, I had the opportunity to work in a number of other kinds of environments. For example, I was a deputy director of the Florida Department of Law Enforcement; undersheriff of two county police departments: the San Francisco County Sheriff's Office and the Orange County Florida Sheriff's Office; chief of police in a city of 15,000 people; and a patrolman in Corvallis, Oregon, an area that had perhaps 136 blacks in the entire county. I was also assistant police chief of Savannah, Georgia. As you can see, I have had an opportunity to work in a variety of communities in the West and in the South, in all-white communities for all practical purposes, and in a community like Charleston with 41 percent minorities.

These experiences have given me a perspective that some police administrators do not have. It has caused me to look at the world in a much wider fashion than I would have otherwise. What I thought was impossible when I was a local law enforcement officer, I found being done all the time in state law enforcement. What we thought we could not do in state law enforcement, for fear of stepping on the toes of local law enforcement officers, I found was being done all the time by local law enforcement officers themselves.

It is my contention that the office of the chief of police is the most important office in the municipality except for that of the mayor or city manager. There is more interest—media interest, community interest, council interest—in the filling of that one position than there would be for, say, the fire chief or parks director or planning director.

CHANGING POLITICAL ENVIRONMENT

I was selected as chief of police from about 250 applicants for the job. For many people in the city, my appointment was not the same type of issue that it would have been if I had been a Caucasian. In the case of Anglos, the dispute or argument, if there is any in the community, is focused on whether the particular person is the best one for the job. But as a minority group person, the issue was different. In my case, they asked whether or not I was *capable*, because I am black. Even though I had the skill, the intelligence, the knowledge, and the background, the question was still whether I was even qualified to perform the job. In any case, I was appointed chief of police. I was under no illusions and recognized the significance of my appointment in a place like Charleston, South Carolina, the birthplace of the Confederacy, the home of Fort Sumter—where the first shots of the Civil War were fired.

Charleston was the kind of city that was so parochial that despite the fact that the prior chief was there for twelve years, the day after his death a local paper stated the "new" chief is dead. That was after twelve years! The city was founded nearly 316 years ago. It takes a long time to work your way in. Before I was appointed, there were some political changes that shifted the political environment in Charleston. If you look at every single city in the United States with a minority chief executive or a minority chief in the police department, you will find that there were some political things that happened first. Almost none of these people got appointed simply because they were qualified; I certainly did not.

About three or four years before I arrived, Charleston adopted single member district representation. The city was divided into twelve different districts, which made it possible for the city council to be composed of six whites and six blacks. (Among that total of twelve people there were also four women.) The city council went from the one token black person to a situation where blacks had substantial power and influence. However, nothing could be done unless at least one of the white council persons agreed with them and vice versa. Therefore, the situation mandated cooperation. Our city has changed from one where minorities and women had very little participation in government to one of substantial participation. I am certainly not naive enough to believe

THE NEW SLEUTH

that I would have been chosen chief of police, even if I was the best qualified, if these changes had not occurred.

When it was announced that I was appointed police chief in 1982, people were, of course, stunned. It not only blew minds in the Anglo community, but it also blew a lot of people's minds in the black community. A group of ministers had gone to the mayor six months before, when the previous chief had died, and said, "When you consider appointing a new chief, we would like you also to consider qualified minorities." They expected the mayor to do precisely that—consider a qualified minority to be chief, then sit down and decide on somebody else. They expected that even if that much was done, it would have been more than had ever been done before. The mayor had political courage, no question about it, and took a political risk. I was appointed chief of police.

COMMUNITY RECEPTION

I wondered what kind of reception I would get from the men and the women of the department, and from people in general. I got a little hint of what it might be, because the same week that I was appointed chief of police, Lee Brown was appointed chief of police of my hometown, Houston, Texas. He was met with a city council of about sixteen members, and was able to get only twelve votes to confirm him in that position. I was met with a city council of twelve members and got twelve votes to confirm me, so that was a little different.

At the formal reception held after I was sworn in, I was greeted by people from all walks of the community. Senator Hollings flew down from Washington to be there and I was sworn in by the chief municipal judge, also a black. A rabbi led the invocation. Many other politicians—the lieutenant governor, the secretary of state—also came to Charleston. This really was a big event in South Carolina. I had been chief in other places and had never had this much attention. Obviously they were there to see me, and I was very humble. I did not know what to say or what to do, but Lee Brown did not have the same situation. He had an outfit called the Ku Klux Klan at his reception, parading outside. Now, certainly coming to South Carolina, one would expect that same thing might occur. It did not happen. As a matter of fact, during the years I have been chief of police, I have received nothing but tremendous support from the city council and the mayor, and all segments of the community have given me an opportunity to do my job. There are a lot of unrealistic expectations, however.

In the first place, many people in the white community thought that somehow if we have a black chief of police, maybe black criminals will not commit so many crimes. People said that on radio and television programs. I said this is insane! Does it logically follow that if you have a white chief of police, whites will not commit so many crimes? Of course, that was ridiculous. On the other hand, there were blacks who felt that "he is going to be chief of the blacks, and he will not be chief of the whites. He will tell us what to do, but he will not tell anybody else what to do. The whites will do what they have always done, and he will just be there with a name and a title but no authority."

Yet there was one thing that everybody was absolutely sure about, except the mayor, who was the only one not sharing this position. The black community and the white community were certain that I would not last six months. You could get a bet on me anywhere in the community. I must say the soul brothers gave me three months longer than most of the whites did. Consequently, people did not really begin to take me seriously, until it looked like I was going to be there for a while. As a matter of fact, one of the local chiefs called me up and said, "Hey, it looks like you are going to be here for a while now." This was after about four or five months, and he wanted to have lunch. This expectation was not without basis on their part. They had a chief in another local department the year before, who lasted six months, but he was incompetent.

EXPECTATIONS

People said, "Those white guys aren't going to work for you. This is the South, they never worked in their lives for a black guy." In our department, we had two black sergeants, two black captains, and no black lieutenants. The other officers never really paid any attention to the black sergeants or the black captains, because if they did not like an order those guys gave, they went around them, went to their chief and the chief changed the order. With a black guy as chief, however, they believed that these two captains were going to be in the driver's seat, so to speak. People had very unrealistic expectations.

Many whites felt that, because I was black, I was going to be easy on black criminals; many black criminals thought that, too. Many people felt that it was simply not going to be a successful social experiment having a black chief of police. Other persons, and I resented them more than all the others, felt that somehow they were going to get behind me and join in the crusade, just as they had joined in the bus boycotts. They believed I was the kind of person who needed them standing out in front of me beating away various kinds of adversaries, that I could not stand on my own two feet. I thought this was terrible since I had a demonstrated record of success in law enforcement administration.

Minorities inside the department felt that they had it made now. Some said, "We can do whatever we want to do, we will get all the new promotions and good assignments because we got a brother in there." Minorities outside the department felt that the end of police brutality was at hand. That from this day forward, not one policeman would step out of line again, because we got a brother in there. We had a lot of whites who felt that no white man would ever be promoted in this department again. We had some people outside the department who felt that Charleston had gone to the dogs now, so they thought that Caucasians were going to leave the department. In fact, nobody left the department at all for six months, and when people finally did leave, they were retiring after more than thirty years of service. These were officers who had put in for their retirement before they even knew who the chief of police was going to be. The only thing people in the department knew was that the chief was going to come from outside. Another reason why people did not leave was the department pays the highest salary of any law enforcement agency in the state, by thousands of dollars. So anybody who left for another job would have to be really committed to racism, because it would cost thousands of dollars.

The department is a southern police department, and it is a paramilitary unit. The ranks in the department are very similar to ranks in the military—sergeant, staff sergeant, etc. When a lieutenant comes to my office—that is the lowest commissioned rank—he stands at attention, and I say "at ease" because that is the way it is done in Charleston. After the Civil War, the U.S. Army was the police in Charleston. The military set up the police in Charleston along the same lines as the military. When the army left after 1878, I think it was, it left that legacy. It is quite different than some departments in Florida, San Francisco, and other places. The chief's position in Charleston was looked upon as a high position in city government. The department has a formal inspection every year in which all the officers line up, and the mayor, city council, and chief of police inspect the ranks. Now you would think that this structure would make it very difficult to change the operation, but the exact opposite was the case. It made it very easy, because if you gave an instruction, it was followed. I have never been challenged in my authority as to who runs the department. During my administration, only three officers have gone to the mayor, usually because they did not get merit pay. It didn't do them any good. More significantly, my authority to run the police department has never been challenged.

ADMINISTRATIVE PHILOSOPHY

My first administrative test came three days into the job. No matter how skilled you are as an administrator, there is such a thing as bad luck. If that phone rings at 3:00 A.M. and you pick it up to hear that a white police officer has shot and killed a fifteen-year-old black female quadriplegic, you have had bad luck. I mean that is bad luck, not just for the officer and the poor person who was killed, but certainly for the chief of police as well. That did not happen to me—what happened to me was something less, so I had good luck!

There was a mini-confrontation between some warrant officers and some people in the housing project, and the police officers were accused of using excessive force. I came into the department with a reputation of cracking down and stopping excessive force in the previous departments where I had worked. The officers were also accused of verbally abusing people through cursing and using racial epithets. Everybody was waiting with bated breath to see what would happen in my very first case.

The day before this incident, a local police chief came and said, "Let me tell you something, whatever you do, stay away from the news media. They're nothing but trouble—stay away from them." I knew right then that he obviously had not the foggiest notion of being a minority group person in a position like mine. He could stay away from the news media and hide somewhere, but there was no way that the first black police chief of Charleston, South Carolina, the birthplace of the Confederacy, would be able to hide from the news media. People from all over the country were looking to see what would happen.

After my personal investigation and talking with people in the neighborhood, I concluded that no excessive force had been used against the citizens. People in my department will tell you that there are two groups that I never believe at face value: One group is the criminal element. Why? Because they have lied to me so many times. The second group is police officers. Why? Because they have lied to me so many times. So I investigated.

What I found was that the officers had used racial insults when they were trying to control the people. It was the use of racial insults which caused three criminals, for which there were arrest warrants for serious crimes—armed robbery, burglary—to be given support from people in the community. In other words, those two cops were successful in giving three criminals, who were arrested repeatedly, support from the large majority of the people in the neighborhood who were not criminals. That is how smart they were. So I realized that my job in the city was to rob the criminal element of the support given by law-abiding people in the community.

How was I going to do that? In two ways: In the community and in the police department. First, I had to de-racialize the perception of crime in this city. Just because you happen to be black and happen to live in the black community, you are not a criminal. Between 96 or 97 percent of the black community do not break any laws whatsoever, except maybe rolling through an occasional stop sign at 3:00 A.M. That is the most they are ever going to do. So why alienate them from the police department? You can de-racialize crime by making police officers aware that there is a distinction between the citizens and the criminal element.

I was lucky in another way as well. I suspended the officers for using profanity, but I did not suspend them for using racial insults—I will tell you why in a minute. I suspended them for doing it against three crooks who were real garbage. That set the level of my intolerance all the way down to the guy who had no political clout whatsoever. If I had suspended the officers for cursing at a relative of the mayor or the governor, that would not have meant anything; people would have expected that to be done. But here is a guy with no political clout, a criminal, no question about it. When you cannot be profane with the lowest guy—who has no influence, no clout, no money, no nothing—then everybody else higher than that level is protected. In that department, it was a common practice to curse at people, and to me that was insane.

Many said, "Give them a second chance," but I am one of those persons who believes in fairness, justice, and equity. Whatever you do in one situation, the question is are you going to do that in all the other similar situations? At that time, the department had about 216 sworn officers, and I said if I give these two guys a second chance, that means that I have got to give the other 214 officers a second chance. Someone could say, "Well, he did it and you gave him a second chance, well how can you be any different with me?" You say, "I am not going to tolerate any more!" So I nail them the first time. They were wrong. I had them by the short hairs because they were wrong. There was no employee group or anywhere else they could go where somebody would say that it was the right thing to do. Everybody would have to conclude that no matter how much they had been provoked, they were wrong. There would be nobody who would say that it was proper police behavior. In the last four years, I have had to nail only one other person for cursing. No one has to ask what Greenberg is going to do if one of my officers curses at somebody. All they have to do is ask the guys who got suspended.

Finally, I looked at it this way. We are paying those guys about $26,000 to $27,000 a year. Why should I pay somebody $27,000 a year to curse at citizens? It simply gives criminals allies that they should not have, it generates ill will toward the police department, and it contributes nothing to the law enforcement process. There are four words a police officer can utter, and I guarantee you it cannot be topped in any community—"You are under arrest!" When a police officer says that, he has maxed out. All the guy's buddies on the street corner know who has won, and everybody else knows who ultimately won that encounter. These four words can cancel out a chorus of *M.F.*s and *S.O.B.*s.

I said I did not get them because of racial reasons. At that early point

I did not want to racialize what was basically an incident that rose out of officers trying to do their jobs. It was more important simply to zero in on the cursing, which even they recognized was less serious than calling somebody a racial name. I heard about it three days later. "Boy, you should hear what the guys are saying in the squad room. If he suspended somebody for calling somebody a profanity, what in the world would that S.O.B. do if somebody called somebody a nigger?" You know, that let me know that I had had the effect that I wanted. They realized that would be one of the worst things they could do.

When I came to the department, we had an average of three complaints every week against police officers for excessive force. Since I have been in the department, we have had twelve complaints of excessive force. Twelve times somebody has come in and said officers have used excessive force. Of those twelve times, the department agreed with them seven times. Police abuse of citizens is not a political issue in the city of Charleston. Nobody is going to get elected on that issue. I catch no heat from any member of the city council over the issue of excessive force.

We have procedures to make it difficult for officers to use excessive force. We set up a process in which an officer has to report the force that he used before he goes off duty. People do not have to file complaints against the police if officers have to handle someone physically. It is going to be investigated automatically. The officer is locked into his story before he leaves work, before he knows if anybody else was watching, or how many witnesses there were looking through the blinds at what was going on in the street. So, the only option that he really has is to tell the truth, and in those twelve cases, the officers told exactly what they did. It was on file before the people came and complained.

We investigate an officer assaulting someone in the same way the police investigate if someone else was to assault a private citizen. The fact that it is a policeman makes no difference. We go out and investigate it on a criminal basis. If an officer uses excessive force, lies about it, and I find out, I am personally going to arrest him, take him right to the same room where he has rolled the fingerprints of all the other crooks that he has arrested, and put him in front of the same camera to have his picture taken.

In 1981, the year before I became chief, the department arrested 3,100 people. Last year the department arrested 8,256 people, because I am arrest oriented. I make arrests myself. Last year I made twenty-seven arrests—from burglary to indecent exposure, disorderly conduct, drunkenness on the street, drunk driving, and armed robbery. I give them no second chances. You tell him to move on and he does not move on, it's jail time. No second chance. This has convinced people in the city that we can protect them. Now, what does that yield? Confidence to walk the streets and greater support for the police department. I have never asked the Charleston City Council for an additional police officer without getting it. Not many chiefs can tell you that.

In some departments, grievances are resolved by each side choosing a person to serve on a committee. This procedure sets up an adversarial situation. I did not want an adversary situation; all I want is the truth. So we have various kinds of department boards or committees which decide issues, from accidents to discharges of firearms within the department. But I am the one who sets the punishment. They find the facts, I set the punishment. I am the one who says, "You're fired," or "You're suspended," or "You're getting a written reprimand, or oral reprimand." Since I am going to be the one to take the heat from the people outside, I am going to decide how the officers should be punished. I tell the people of Charleston: "If a police officer abuses you, and nothing is done about it, blame me because I am the only guy here who can do something about it."

As we have with the community, we insist that our officers be honest. We arrested one of our officers not long ago for drunk driving. About two years ago, we arrested another one for drunk driving. For cocaine possession, we do not suspend them; we arrest them. When someone says, "Hey, so and so is snorting cocaine," we go through the same procedure we would with any other garbage on the street. We do not tolerate people who do the same thing that they arrest other people for doing, because the worst form of hypocrisy is to put other people in jail for doing exactly the same thing you are doing yourself.

The department, particularly the supervisors, have adopted my management style, and I have taken advantage of the military orientation of the department. When something goes wrong, somebody is responsible. It is not just one of those things. I am the first person the people in the community are going to hold responsible. I cannot say, "Well, folks, he killed a guy, but it was just one of those things." So the person who is responsible is the commanding sergeant and corporal. The man who committed the offense is responsible only if the sergeant and the corporal have done their jobs. If your man does something wrong, I do not want to talk to him, I want to talk to you. Once I am sure that you have met your responsibilities, then I am interested in talking to him. I say, "You're responsible, or he did it on his own. Which way?" He said, "He did it on his own." I say, "Well, proceed with charges against him." I have twenty-six sergeants, forty-four corporals, ten lieutenants, three captains, and two majors watching out for what is going on.

I was in Jerusalem for a trip in 1986, and when I came back a guy had a ten-day suspension for a violation of the department rules and regulations. The suspension was already over before it was even brought to my attention. There wasn't any need to wait for me, because they know what I would do. Do you have any idea how many grievances were filed with the City Grievance Board against our department in the last four years? One grievance, and that person lost. This approach is not creating an adversarial relationship between the officers in the department, because if they do their jobs, I am going to protect them. If they try to do their jobs but screw up in good faith, I am going to protect them. We are going to circle the wagons, say "We're sorry, he made a mistake, but at the time he made the decision, these were the facts that were known to him. Based upon those facts, the decision was reasonable." But if it starts out wrong and the officer is not doing his job, we will nail him.

In the last six years, officers have fired their weapons in the line of duty three times. One guy was killed about five years ago when he pointed a target pistol at police officers. There was no issue about the shooting. Can you imagine shooting a black guy, in a black neighborhood, ten o'clock at night with hundreds of people on the street, and there was no riot, no lawsuit. All the witnesses said the officer told him to drop the gun, one witness said he did not drop the gun, he pointed the gun at the cop. Another witness said he aimed the gun at the cop. Another witness said he raised the gun to the cop. The guy was shot six or seven times by three officers who were present. That is when people know you have no alternative.

If I was to give my management philosophy a name, it would be democratic centralism. Most of you are familiar with Lenin, Welsh from the John Birch Society, and Trotsky. All of them had something in common, and that was decision making by process of democratic centralism. The idea of democratic centralism works like this: Before a decision is made, everybody or anybody has the right to put in his two cents, either by coming to the chief's office or writing a letter to that particular board or commission of the department that is handling the question. But once the decision is made, we do not permit anybody to violate it. You cannot remain in the department and work against a decision that has been made. You have to leave the department to do that. If your particular position loses out, you have lost. You are expected to put your shoulder to the wheel and push along with everybody else until they see that that policy is not working.

We do everything essentially by committee. For example, we use a committee process to determine merit pay allocations. Merit pay is not for doing your job; it is not for those persons who go just beyond the bare minimum that is necessary to keep from getting fired. In our department, usually about 40 percent of the people receive merit pay. All employees will get cost-of-living increases, but merit pay is special. How do we make that decision? What are the factors we use? We set up a committee to make that determination, and I told them that seniority would be used last. Other things had to be equal before seniority was a factor at all. I insisted on that because I am not a seniority-oriented individual. Seniority is good for deciding who is going to have the third week off in October for vacation, but not to decide who gets promoted, who is going to be the boss, or who is going to be transferred to what assignment. It is performance that counts. They came up with a series of steps for merit allocations that were extremely strict, much stricter than the ones that I would have instituted, and they went unchallenged.

I said previously that we had one grievance filed in the last four years. Within our system, disciplinary hearings are handled by a board; e.g., Discharge of Firearms Board or an Accident and Safety Board, thus the only possible reason that a complaint would ever go to the grievance board would be on an appeal of the punishment that I imposed. The guilty ruling is not appealed because they were found guilty by their peers. In the last six years we have had about three discharges of firearms at human beings, and we also shot three dogs. The board decided that in each of these three separate incidences involving dogs that the officers should not have shot the dogs. If I had said that, the officers would have complained—the chief wants us to get bitten. There was no argument or anything else. They said, "You should not have shot that dog." Some of these are people who have worked in the department for twenty-five years, and never fired a shot, so they know the job can be done without shooting at any living thing.

In our department, when somebody does something that he should not have done—whether it is a discharge of a firearm or an accident or some stupid vehicle pursuit that made no sense—we ask whether or not the rules and regulations of the department should be modified in order to deal with similar situations. In the three cases where we shot at human beings—killing one—they decided that the rules and regulations did not need to be changed or modified. If there is a minority report, it has to be put in writing. I want to know the reasons why the minority decided to vote the other way. After the third shooting of an animal by police officers, they decided that the rules and regulations of the department should be changed. They recommended that it be made more difficult for them to shoot animals in those kinds of situations. I accepted the recommendations.

I believe that the closer you get to the people actually performing the job, the higher the quality of the decision-making process. By quality I mean the practicality that it will work. When somebody comes to me, I never say, "Well, we can't do that." I question: "How can we do that? Now, remember we've got to do this and this at the same time; how can we fit this into that? You brought the problem, you solve it." They sometimes refer to me as a Toyota man, you know, "You ask for it, you got it." You fit it in and write it in the format that we have to use, so all I have to do is read it, strike things out, and then have it retyped for my signature. They do not come to me with various kinds of problems. We have a large mounted patrol in the city. They set up their own rules and regulations and I adopted them into the department's procedural orders. What happens if an animal steps on somebody's foot or somebody gets kicked, or whether they can fire from horseback or not, or use batons, all kinds of things. If they violate the rules, they have not violated the chief's rules, they have violated their own rules. The marine patrol section, boat patrol, has its own rules, as do the canine officers and the SWAT team. Therefore, when somebody does not adhere to the rules, it is not a rule that was imposed by the chief. These are rules that are adopted by the police department and by the people who are doing that type of work. As a result, there is hardly any basis for any kind of grievance being filed because these rules and regulations were decided by peers doing the same kind of work under the same kind of conditions.

Democratic centralism was a welcome change. Previously, decisions were made at the top, and this management change was very disconcerting for the number-two man of the department. He had been brought into the department through the Marine Corps by the previous chief, and had been involved in every single decision that was made. But suddenly, after I arrived, there would be a procedural order regarding department operations on his desk, signed by the chief of police, and he had minimal knowledge and minimal participation. It really upset him. The problem is he had never ridden a horse in his life or performed in any of the other areas, thus, he knew nothing about their particular procedures. I have been a mounted patrol officer, so I know that work. Before that work, I had been a marine patrol officer, so I know what that work is. Let the people who have that particular job function help determine what it is.

Everyone has to adhere to the rules. Once I had a traffic accident in a department-owned vehicle, and I went before the Accident and Safety Board, just like any of the officers who have a traffic accident, and I had to explain what I was doing at the time of the accident. It was a very clear situation. They do not issue any punishment to me or anybody else; they only find the facts. There was the chief sitting there, and the other guy sat at the opposite side of the table. Luckily for me, there were no issues of fact in the case. I was simply telling them exactly what happened. The other person had admitted fault, but everybody has to go to the board, regardless of his rank. The rules apply to everybody, and the officers like that.

INNOVATIONS AND SUCCESSES

Each September, we have an annual department meeting with two guidelines: First, anybody who is not on duty can come, and we have it at about four o'clock in the afternoon. Second, nobody above the rank of sergeant, except me, can come to the meeting. I did not set that rule; the officers set it. They did that because they felt that the presence of lieutenants, captains, and majors would hinder communication. I have found in my experience that the new ideas, new ways of doing things and procedures that really can help the department move forward come from the lower-ranking people of the department. They come very often from people who have worked in the police department for the least amount of time, because they have not been there long enough to believe the established way is the only way to do it.

These meetings give me an opportunity to interact with the officers and take notes. They ask me questions about anything they want, any disciplinary decision that was made that they are interested in, why it was made that way, why squads are set the way they are. There is nothing that is off limits. They can also make any kind of proposal or recommendation that they want. Often, I say, "I should have thought of that myself. Here's a guy who's buck private, working out in a patrol car, and he thought of something like that. That's a fantastic idea! I should have thought of that myself." What I find most often is when I ask them, "Do you want me to do it, and give you the credit for it, or do you just want me to do it?" the response is, "Chief, just do it." That indicates to me that he has already brought the idea up to some lieutenant or captain who shot it down before it even got to me.

We have instituted a program in the city with foot patrol officers, called "Take Back the Streets." Criminals may decide to go out at three or four o'clock in the morning. They do not worry about getting mugged or somebody robbing them. I say, "You know, that is crazy. These guys are criminals and whenever they want to go out, they go out. Two o'clock in the morning, or two in the afternoon, they do not consider the fact that it is dangerous out there. But citizens are afraid to leave their homes after nine o'clock." I said, "Let's give the criminals a little heat." So we set up this foot patrol program in neighborhood areas and in downtown areas—a very intensive foot patrol program. The same officer over and over, all the time. He knows the people, they know him. He goes to every meeting of the neighborhood associations. Our city has about forty-five neighborhood associations, so he can find out what is important to these people. Are there special areas of concern that the community would like the officer to pay attention? These meetings are very important to get a sense of the community. People want to be able to walk down the street, at least in the daytime, without being robbed. They expect to come home at night and find that their Sony television is still on the table where they left it. These expectations are not unreasonable.

As I said, we made a distinction between the criminals and the people in the neighborhood. We have mounted a rescue operation to save the people on the east side of the city from the criminal element. It had never been done in Charleston before. They had a crackdown on crime on the east side before, but the police made no distinction between criminals and the people in the neighborhood—they made everybody move. Little old ladies going down the street working in the historic district where all the white folks stayed were safe, and nobody ever snatched purses in that neighborhood. But when they got to their own neighborhood, somebody would snatch their purse and knock them to the street. It is not right for them to be paying Sears, Montgomery Ward, and J. C. Penney's for television sets that were stolen from them two and three years before. We intended to rescue the people on the east side from the criminal element.

When the neighborhood people see the officers on the beat, they will know that they are not there for the safety of the criminals. We know who the criminals are, for they have been arrested time and time again. We know them by name. We tell them, "Hey, beat it." We tell the other people, "Hey, don't go home, you don't have to go home. You don't have to be afraid of me. You're walking in the area, going wherever you're going, so go on about your business." The neighborhood in the worst part of the city of Charleston is safer, and now has a lower crime rate than the neighborhood where the mayor lives.

Last year we had a 22 percent decrease in crime in the city of Charleston. We had the same number of burglaries in 1985 in the city of Charleston as we had in 1959. The city annexed twenty-five square miles during that time, and the city's population grew by 30,000 during that time. Yet we had the same number of break-ins in 1985 as we did in 1959, so it can be done. There is a price to pay. You have to have the political support to do it. I had the political support from the City Council to move them (the criminals).

Now we did not eliminate crime. What we did was move crime out into the other cities, which caused a tremendous increase in crime for them.

We have also changed the image of the foot patrol. Before I came into the department, foot patrol was punishment. Now we select people on the basis of their youth. Foot patrol is not a job for an old man; it is a job for a young man. In our department, if you are over twenty-seven years old, you are really too old for foot patrol; you are too old to be out on the street chasing criminals. Our officers do not wear nice, shiny military shoes. They wear running shoes. We wanted to get the criminals off the street and many of them are between the ages of fifteen and twenty-five. Therefore, we needed to put officers on the street who, if the criminal ran, would have a good chance to catch him. You have to have officers with the proper equipment, who can run a guy down the street, go over the back fence, under the house if necessary, up the steps, kick in the door, follow right behind him through the hall, and up the stairs into the bathroom where he is holding the door trying to keep you out. However, to accomplish this, you also must have the backing of the community, so we have set up various ways to make sure that the support is forthcoming.

When you knock somebody's door in, people get upset. If a mother comes home from work to find her door broken in, she is not going to say, "Well, Jimmy stole something out of the store and ran. The police ran after him and he tried to go in the house and slam the door. The police forced the door open, arrested him, and took him to jail." That is what happened, but that is not what she is going to say. Mama is going to say, "Who broke my door? The police!" So when we break a door, we fix the door—immediately. I have my own carpenters who work full time for the police department. They go out, and they repair that particular door. We tell them, "We're sorry, but this guy came running into your place, and we had to get him out for you." What the residents are worried about is that they cannot secure their property and are afraid to leave their homes. They have no money to fix the door. The program costs me about $2,000 a year worth of materials and costs me nothing in labor. Our carpenters have police radios in their trucks, so they can come out at 2:00 A.M., if needed, to fix that door so that property is left secure and the person will feel the police did a favor. The same principle applies to other property damaged in pursuit.

One of the successes that I have had in the city was in convincing people that tough law enforcement and police brutality were not synonymous. We convinced men in the department that if we stopped police brutality, increasing assaults against police officers would not be the result. We now have fewer assaults against police officers than we have ever had and the highest number of arrests in the history of the city. The city has never been bigger, the police department has never been larger, and it has never been better paid. We simply convinced the people in the city that we can protect them. Before they did not believe that—they just did not believe that we actually had the investigative skill or the physical ability to protect them.

I am a person who maintains that it does absolutely no good for a police officer to come out with a ballpoint pen and a form to fill out about somebody having raped you or busted your head. Moreover, simply going out and getting the guy and arresting him is not enough since the person is still beaten upside the head or is still raped. The idea is to confront known criminals *before* they engage in criminal activities. Now that is really protecting people, though it is not easy to do. In this regard, we have instituted flying squads. Flying squads have nothing to do with airplanes; it is a term that the British use for squads who do not work in police districts, but rather operate all over the city. These are people who know the criminal element in particular areas. We put a black officer and a white officer together and they serve as our only two-man teams in cars.

Why do I put a black officer and a white officer together? Because they are confronting criminal types who at that particular moment are not committing crimes. They might say, "Hello, Jimmy baby, what you got in that bag you're carrying?" You would be surprised at the number of people who will drop the bag and start running when a uniformed police officer asks them, "What you got in that bag?" A police officer, just like anybody else, has the right to stop someone in the street and ask them a question. There is nothing illegal about that. The problem comes in when the person refuses to answer that question. We have the black officer and the white officer together, because that combination de-racializes the conflict. Whatever conflict there is has nothing to do with race. It relates only to the merits of the stop/frisk by itself and nothing else.

These guys, unfortunately, are selected on the basis of their ability to run and their ability to fight, because that is what you have to do in these kinds of situations. Actually, they fight very rarely, because if you are prepared to fight, you usually do not have to fight. In a three-month period, the flying squads were involved in 98 foot chases and they caught the guys 93 times. That is credibility not just for them but for the whole department. People believe that we can protect them. That is the reason why I have never asked the Charleston City Council for a police officer and not gotten it. We have no opposition to our budget. I have only been to two city council meetings in four years. Once when I was sworn in and once when I had about six guys retiring from the department who had worked for twenty-five, forty, or forty-five years. We have shown what we can do with the money. We are not going to oppress the people of the city, we are going to go after the criminal element and those arrest statistics I gave you are indicative of that, but we are not going to abuse people. I think the fact that we have convinced people that we can protect them is one of my major successes.

Another success I have had is an agreement that the Charleston police will be the highest paid law enforcement officers in the state of South Carolina. Other departments have tried to rise to our level, but we will never have to worry about coming to where they are, even if we have to tax ourselves to do it. Foot patrol is very expensive. I did not take guys out of cars and put them on foot patrol. Those were all new positions that the city taxed itself for.

A final success concerns relations with the city prosecutor. I do not have any argument with the prosecutors of the city of Charleston because I help hire them. I let prosecutors drive an unmarked vehicle to and from work and wherever they are going. The mayor believes that we are not going to be successful unless the prosecutor has the support of the officers in the department and officers have the support of the prosecutor. If they fight as they did before I came to the department—the prosecutor against the police—there is only one group in the city that benefits: the criminal element. The best way to make sure that the prosecutor is compatible with the police department is to have the police department select that particular person. You have to be a lawyer to be a prosecutor, but that person must also understand the joy of making an arrest. Our prosecutors always are ex-FBI agents or police officers because they understand what making an arrest and going through that door is. They have done it themselves.

PREPARATION AND LESSONS LEARNED

When a minority group person has the opportunity for a position such as chief of police, there is an expectation in some quarters that things will be better for minority group people in the service delivery system than they were before. And, of course, other people feel everything is going to go to hell and everything is going to be terrible with that person holding that particular position. And I have seen both situations happen. I think perceptions are of great importance.

If a minority administrator simply follows in the footsteps of the person who preceded him, then it really does not make any difference whether a minority person holds that position. Because we are minority people, I think we have a perspective that is much broader than that of people who have not had our experiences. If we are going to simply replace an Anglo administrator who perhaps was insensitive with a minority administrator who is equally insensitive, then I do not see any gain relative to anyone in the system other than to that one individual. As minority group people, we have to do more than just simply provide an increased income or increased influence for ourselves because, whether we like it or not, there is no way that we can separate ourselves from the activities of other minorities. Whether it is justified or not, all of us, from our respective minority groups, are sometimes, at least privately, embarrassed and ashamed when a person of our particular minority group does something that is derogatory to our group. We may not articulate it, but we read the newspaper, hear it on the radio, watch it on television—we are a little embarrassed within ourselves. Likewise, when a minority person, particularly of our particular ethnic group, does something that is noteworthy in society, our chests fill with pride. We are very happy to see that this person has won the Nobel Prize or some other very worthwhile award or gained some prestigious position.

I once discussed this with a friend of mine who is an Anglo, and he said that as far as he was concerned, if another Anglo did something, it was strictly an individual achievement. He does not tie his star to anything good that some other person from his group does or become diminished because of anything bad. He is free from the stigma that minorities have had to suffer for so long relative to negative stereotypes. If another Anglo does something wrong, it has nothing to do with him. He does not worry about what people are going to think about him at work or how people are going to view his capabilities.

An illustrative example of this phenomenon is something that happened to me when I was a police officer in Florida. I heard a woman scream one night when I was putting up my lawn mower. It sounded like it came from about a block and a half away. I immediately ran in the house and got my gun. I was in shorts and flip-flops and did not even have my badge. I got in the car and drove to where I thought the scream came from. A teenager had snatched a woman's purse and had struck her with his fist several times in the process. As soon as I arrived, she recognized me as the chief of police of that municipality and she was screaming and yelling that "it was one of your people!" I was trying to figure out how she felt that I had some personal responsibility simply by being black. All she knew was that I had race in common with this particular thief. But I realize, of course, there is nothing I can do about that. Some are going to look at anything I do or anything the thief does and not see a dime's worth of difference between a black chief of police and a black purse snatcher.

Sometimes we overlook the legacy of various minorities in the United States, particularly in the Southwest and in the South. It is not enough for us to do a good job. It is not enough for us to be honest. We must also *appear* honest. We have got to go out of our way to make it abundantly clear that our activities are honorable activities. We cannot simply say, "Well, I'm an honest man and I know that." If you are the only one who knows that, then you are going to be in trouble. An Anglo might be able to be the only one who knows that because he is not going to be under the intense scrutiny that the rest of us are going to be under. In some ways it makes us stronger and better administrators. In other ways, of course, we should not have to meet a higher standard to get even a minor opportunity. But that is, to me, simply the facts of life and, unfortunately, something we are going to have to continue to confront into the future. I do not see it stopping soon.

Another thing I have learned is that some minorities are afraid to be the boss. Therefore, you wind up with the same people running things. These frightened administrators continue to seek their advice in order to make a decision. So little has changed. If you are not going to have changes, as I said earlier, it makes no difference then whether the person in that position is a minority or a nonminority.

Minority administrators must also oppose the exclusion of other minorities and women from access to opportunities. We should not be concerned only with our own particular group. A lot of people feel females and minority group males compete for the same types of positions. I doubt if you will find a person who is more of a male chauvinist than I am. I really doubt that. But on the other hand, if you look at the kind of promotions, recruitment, and assignments in the agency that I had responsibility for, we have women in every job that anybody else is in. Now why would somebody who is raised a male, raised in the United States, in Texas, which has to be the bastion of male chauvinism, be a champion of women? Self-interest.

Self-interest? How? Self-interest because I have never met a person who disliked female police officers, for example, who also did not dislike black police officers. If opponents succeed in keeping out female police officers or Asian police officers or Hispanic police officers, then that is a blow against me as well, even though I do not fall into any of those categories. It is not in my best interest to see somebody lose a job because she is a woman, or not get a job because she is a woman or Hispanic. I gain nothing from that. In fact, I lose because that has made opponents stronger. It may be an Hispanic that they are opposed to today, but tomorrow they may be opposed to a black person like I am. I do not see any way that I can succeed as a minority by building my success on the backs of other minorities or women. It may do me some good as an individual, but if that is all we are looking for, it has no broader meaning. So I provide any kind of assistance that I can on a very, very selfish basis. I have nothing to gain by them being kept out and everything to gain by them participating.

COMMUNITY RELATIONSHIPS

Access for the community is very, very important because it is one significant dimension that differentiates minority administrators from other administrators. Minority administrators provide access for minority people to come to their offices. When I became chief, minorities began to gain the same access to public officials that the whites had enjoyed. The whites did not get less access to the office of the chief deputy sheriff or the chief of police because a minority was in the job. They have maintained that access, but minorities, who do not have money, do not have income, do not have education, began to share in that same access. Providing access is one of the most important responsibilities for minority administrators. Indeed, it is a bare minimum requirement for performance.

I am very committed to affirmative action, which has always been a very touchy subject in the law enforcement community. The catch phrases are that you are lowering the standards in order to bring minorities and women into the field. When I came to the city, I heard rumors that certain people did not like blacks, and you find out who these guys are through the rumor mill. So I said to myself, "Why should I be the only one trying to recruit minorities into the community? These other guys get paid by the city just as I do, and it's official policy of the city of Charleston to seek out minorities in the schools, colleges, military, wherever, and try to attract them to our city government, particularly to the police and fire departments." So I decided to have some of these guys help me. I went and got some of the worst possible rednecks in the department and said, "I want you to bring me one and I want you to do it soon. That's right, that's right. Bring me one. All I want is one, but I want you to bring him and I want you to make sure that the guy is gonna pass all the different tests and procedures. I want you to explain to him what the requirements are and what has to be done."

In our city we have merit pay which is generally a 5 percent increase over your base pay. In order to get merit pay, you have to meet all of your objectives. I told them: "Your objective is to get somebody who is black who can successfully pass the police academy, successfully pass the probationary period, and be a police officer. That is what you have to do. That is your mission." What do you think they did? They each went out and got me one. So suddenly I was not the only one interested in trying to find minorities. One said, "We're lowering standards by doing this." I told him: "If you don't want to lower standards, find somebody who will meet them. Others given the same instructions have been successful." Some of them brought three and four, which put pressure to bring in more as well. Otherwise, they would have failed doubly—not only have failed to meet their mission but failed when other people were succeeding.

Through this procedure we moved from about 17 percent minority to 35 percent minority in the sworn ranks. As a matter of fact, in the last year we abandoned the Affirmative Action Program for civilian employees because we now have approximately 65 percent minorities. In the sworn ranks since the last part of last year, we no longer have an Affirmative Action Program for the lower-level positions. But the ranking positions, everything from corporal up to the chief of police, continue to underrepresent minorities. We are in a lot better shape than we were four or five years ago, but we still have a lot of work to do.

We have the advantage in that we have the ability to go out and hire minority people from other departments. I do not have to train them all from scratch. I can say, "Hey, get more money than you are making someplace else and come over with us." On that basis we have been able to do a lot better than people expected. But as long as you have only the chief of police or only the lieutenant in charge of recruiting and personnel interested in affirmative action, you are not going to succeed.

You have got to get everybody, including the rednecks—if they want to stay, get promotions and merit pay, and be successful—involved in the effort.

We need not only to be concerned with affirmative action at the entry level and in promotions, but also with what I refer to as horizontal affirmative action. When I came to the department, there were positions in the department that were viewed as white people's positions. They were not particularly better paid than others or had more rank or prestige associated with them, for example, crime scene investigation officer or working in the computer center. Blacks said, "Those are for white folk, not for us. Patrol, armed robbery investigation, we can do that, but a crime prevention officer or director of the communication center is not anything we ought to be doing." And, of course, whites agreed. These were jobs that were more managerial in nature. The very thing that made it possible for these people to get promoted later to lieutenant, captain, and major was their experience in these areas of police work. My intent was to make sure that minorities had those opportunities. I did not see anything crazy about a black guy with a microscope in a crime lab trying to make fracture matches after somebody tried to break into a building with a particular tool. They were not going to make any more money doing that but it was an area of expertise that was totally lacking among minorities.

Of course, I put an end to that. I had to push a lot of them, kicking and screaming, into the crime laboratory, communications, records, and data processing. Some of the really technical positions in the department have applications beyond the police department. If you are an armed robbery investigator or a bad check investigator, that does not do you much good anywhere else except in a law enforcement agency. We wanted people with a wide range of skills, so we had to push people and pull them into some of these other areas.

I have not experienced tension between myself or my department and minority communities or minority employees. No employee of this department has filed a grievance during the past four years. The minority (black) community is one of the strongest supporters of the police department.

I do not serve as a spokesman for the black or minority community. I am the leader and spokesman for the police department and handle relations between the police department and all outside agencies or groups. I see myself first as a police administrator, and I lay no claim to any following except that which may exist in the police department.

I belong to and participate in a number of other organizations wherein my presence as a minority group person may have some special significance. However, I do not see that role for me in the police department. I am active in the Heart Association, Cancer Society, Boy Scouts, as well as various religious groups. My activities in these groups are oriented toward the entire community.

GOALS FOR THE MINORITY COMMUNITY

One of the things I try to do, that we all ought to do, is destroy stereotypes as much as we can. We had a couple of incidents that allowed me to do that. There were a series of very bad tornadoes two years ago in South Carolina which literally tore apart the downtown areas of some small towns. People in these law enforcement agencies, which were very small—ten, twelve, fifteen people—were working twenty hours a day, seven days a week. After about five or six days, they were just absolutely exhausted. We volunteered to police those towns so the local officers could have two or three days off.

Some of those towns never had a black in the police department. So whom did we select? We sent a Chinese-American sergeant in charge of the operation and two Hispanic officers. Since I am a black, I know that they expected me to send four, five, six blacks to the town, but I sent only one black. They know we have black officers; they do not need that demonstrated, but we wanted to let them see what kind of diverse environment we had in our city. The only Chinese person they had ever seen before was at the local restaurant. But they could not even conceive of a Chinese person actually being responsible for police enforcement in their city. They were not prepared for that.

We have a very famous mounted patrol force in Charleston. Other jurisdictions like our officers to teach their mounted patrol officers. We received a request to participate in a parade in a city that is way back in the sticks. We sent only six of our mounted patrol officers, which consisted of two women, a Hispanic, two blacks, and a white male. Not only were they just amazed by how well the horses were trained, but to see a black person or a woman controlling the animal's actions just blew their minds. They never expected that particular mounted patrol to show up because in their minds they equated mounted patrol with white guys. It showed the diversity of our department's thinking. We specifically selected that group because we wanted to let them see that our community was different from theirs and was light years ahead of theirs in what was possible and socially acceptable. They are still talking about whether or not a woman should be in law enforcement, where the first black ever to apply for a job is still making news. So we think it is a good opportunity to try to dispel stereotypes and show that minority people are well-established and in both command and supervisory positions in law enforcement.

We have a black female officer who is the only person in the state of South Carolina who deals with child sexual abuse. She is very skilled in using the dolls. We had a situation where a young, white female accused a very rich, rich, rich plantation owner of molesting her, and the police chief in the town did not know what to do. He did not know whether to believe the girl or not. "If we arrest this man and it turns out later there was nothing to it, you know, I'm gone, I'm finished! Can you send me somebody who can talk to this girl and find out what actually took place?" I said I would send the best person I had. The best person is Hazel Giles. When she showed up, I am sure he said, "I'm finished, I'm finished!" The reason that he came to us was he knew we had the best person. He just did not know who that person was. She worked with the child and was able to determine exactly what the man had done and to assist the prosecutor in deciding whether or not to file charges. But it shocked everyone that the man's fate, with all his millions of dollars, might be in the hands of a black woman from the city of Charleston.

The methods I have described are more likely to advance minority goals than other tactics. For example, I do not believe that protest politics should be a major way for blacks as a minority to promote change. Today there are over 6,700 black elected officials, who, in many cases, can make known the desires of blacks for changes in society. This is not true, of course, for all minorities, but I do feel it is true for blacks. In addition, in recent years the courts, even at the state level, have been effectively used as a change agent for the black community. I know of no justification within a country like ours for citizens in the black community as a whole or individually to resort to violence to foster change. I believe that violence in promoting social or economic or political change would be counterproductive.

UNIQUE PROBLEMS/OPPORTUNITIES DUE TO MINORITY STATUS

As a minority group person who is well known in the community, I am sometimes called upon by whites to suggest ways in which the minority community can be urged to participate in community projects. I believe it is an advantage to be a minority when government or other actors plan activities and projects and fail to understand what a minority perspective may be regarding that issue. It has been my experience that ignorance rather than malice is the root cause of most minority group tensions.

8

Phoenix: Progressive Administration in a "Wild West" Environment

Ruben B. Ortega

INTRODUCTION

I became police chief in the city of Phoenix in 1980. Presently, our department consists of 1,750 sworn officers, 500 non-sworn employees, and our annual budget is over $100 million. When I was appointed, the question could have been raised: Who in their right mind would appoint a Hispanic to be police chief of one of the largest cities in the country, currently the ninth largest in the United States? In 1980, many believed that Hispanics were not capable of performing certain jobs. I have to give a lot of credit to the city manager, for he had the courage at that time to appoint me police chief. The mentality existed among some people toward Hispanics that, for example, if they saw a white man driving a white Cadillac that was white power, if they saw a black driving a white Cadillac that was black power, if they saw a Hispanic in a Cadillac it had to be grand theft auto. My appointment was a bold step forward for the city of Phoenix.

SELECTION PROCESS

Before I was appointed, the city had recruited nationally for the position. We had applicants from New York City to California, including a number of applicants from major cities. The list was narrowed down to the top thirteen, and all thirteen of us went through four days of crucial testing. A professional firm was brought in to do the assessments and we were each grilled for four days. At the end of those sessions, we were interviewed by a number of committees, one of which was made up of local citizens the city manager appointed to evaluate what he considered to be the top four or five applicants and to give him a recommendation. I had made up my mind that, first, if it was obvious to me going through the process that I was not qualified, I was going to withdraw. Second, if it looked like I was being carried along because the city needed a minority in a top position, I would not accept the position under those conditions.

Going through the process and being selected, I have to believe that I possessed a little something extra that the city manager recognized. For example, those who applied had similar qualifications in terms of experience and education. We all had college degrees and similar years of police experience in management positions. Everything appeared equal. In some cases some may have even had a little more education than I had—some had master's and one was working toward a doctor's degree. But I had a local advantage and I think the city manager recognized that. I had the advantage of having been observed under fire. I was on the force during the 1960s and early 1970s when most major cities were experiencing serious problems of racial disorder. The city manager, elected officials, and I many times were out in the city trying to put out fires. That was an added advantage because I felt confident that he knew that I was poised under fire.

He was also taking a chance, however, because we still had critics in the city who felt that any major appointment of a minority by a white administrator, particularly for police chief, was simply meant to appease the minority population. I have to believe that entered his mind. If you look across the country today there are advances that have been made by minorities in law enforcement. Many major cities now have minority police chiefs: Chicago, Detroit, New York, Baltimore, Washington, D.C., Houston, Atlanta, Phoenix, and San Antonio.

Going through the ranks in the Phoenix Police Department, being involved in dealing with the civil disorders that we were experiencing, I learned that city officials have great concern about civil unrest in their cities. They constantly strive to prevent race riots or disturbances that result in confrontations between police and minorities. I think this has been an impetus for Anglo administrations to appoint minorities to high-level positions. Minorities provided that little extra. They look at it as an insurance policy. If we do have a demonstration or a riot, we have someone in a position of authority who minorities may trust and therefore will serve to help alleviate the problems. Although that may have been part of the reason for the initial appointments of minority police chiefs in major cities, those appointed knew that they had the experience and the knowledge to do a good job. Once in, they proved without a doubt that they could handle the job.

Although racial incidents have not been totally prevented, the violent aftermath of police-minority confrontations have subsided significantly. It was not uncommon in past years when a police officer killed or seriously injured a member of a minority group, that particular neighborhood erupted in further violence. For days afterwards, police enforcement in the area would be greatly increased. The presence of minority police officials in top positions has allowed minority citizens to take a wait-and-see attitude before reacting and/or making accusations, allowing police officials more time to resolve the incident.

POTENTIALLY EXPLOSIVE SITUATION

A couple of years ago I experienced an incident in our city that all police chiefs dread. I received a telephone call from one of our black police commanders and he said, "Chief, we've got a problem. An officer has just shot a black, unarmed teenager in one of our housing projects and a large crowd is gathering at the scene." In thinking ahead of the worst possible consequences, I remember asking him, "I hope you are going to tell me a minority officer is involved." He said, "No sir, it wasn't. It is an Anglo officer."

I recall going to the scene of the shooting and encountering a black minister who came up to me and said, "What can I do to help?" Together we went into the housing project and spoke to numerous residents who had gathered and told them, "Look, we don't know completely what has happened yet. We have some basic information. We know a young man has been shot. He's been shot by a white officer, and we're going to get to the bottom of it, and we're going to get back to you." In addition, I introduced them to a high-level police commander who I placed in charge of the investigation.

Shortly thereafter, I received numerous calls from minority leaders who did not call to complain or demand an investigation or make other demands, but simply and sincerely stated, "How can we help?" What would have been the response had the chief been Anglo? Hopefully, the same response I received. But I believe there existed a latent feeling of trust toward us that partially was due to my being a minority.

There have been major strides in the selection of minorities for upper-management positions and not just in law enforcement. The doors have opened and many more opportunities will exist for those who are willing to work hard and demonstrate their abilities to do the job. It will not be easy. For every qualified minority there will be many nonminority persons with the *same* qualifications seeking those positions. But I believe that extra dimension that minorities possess will enable minorities to compete, be successful, and contribute to reaching the goal of equal representation in top management positions. But I would caution you on this: do not let us down. There are some who will continue to evaluate and monitor your abilities, searching for weaknesses that justify their beliefs that selection was made mostly on race or ethnic considerations. I am constantly being evaluated, not on the basis of whether I am an effective police chief but on whether I am an effective minority police chief.

ADMINISTRATIVE PHILOSOPHY

I utilize what I call the "team style" of management in the police department, and I instituted it. Prior to my appointment, we had the old autocratic style in which decisions were made on the third floor, sent down the line, and the decisions were just carried out. My style calls for participatory management. Let me suggest to you how this system works and what it is about. Team style management seeks participation from everyone, or at least from a representative of each group of people who would be affected by whatever decision we are going to make. For example, when I have a serious disciplinary decision to make because an officer has gotten into trouble, we need to determine what should the discipline be and to what degree should we carry it out. I bring in my executive staff (five assistant chiefs), share all the facts, and we discuss the matter. I solicit each one's opinion and recommendations as to what the department should do. It is not a decision by committee, and it is not a decision by vote with the majority winning. It is strictly a situation in which I ask them to give me opinions. I want to know what they think. A free sharing of ideas widens the data base for me to make a decision. After I get input from five different people and know how they feel about the situation, then I am in a better position to make a decision. Through this process I have gotten not only the pros but the cons as well.

In other management issues we try to use this process all the way down to the patrolman's level. I tell my assistant chiefs, "Do the same thing with your majors," and we tell the majors, "Do the same thing with your captains." Solicit their input. We resolve a lot of issues and we make a lot of decisions by having committees involved. For example, we were going to institute a new transfer policy a while back, and we formed a committee, headed by a major and composed of patrol officers, sergeants, lieutenants, and captains. Their charge was to give us recommendations on a transfer policy—here are the problems we have encountered, but we think we can do it better; give us some input. They researched it, then they gave me a report with a number of recommendations. They listed them in priority order. I examined them, and picked out what I thought was the best way for us to go. I had input from everybody that would have to be involved. The team style of management has worked well in our department.

It was not easy to implement this style of management, however, because there was resistance from some older officers, who said, "Why do you want to change?" Or, the comment I heard was, "You don't really want our involvement. You're just saying that, but all the decisions will be at the top. We won't see any involvement." In order to convince them of my sincerity, we brought in a consultant, and he put on a workshop. Every member of the department went through that management workshop, from patrolman all the way up to me. It was a workshop on the techniques of how to implement participatory management, how to get people involved, how to convince them that we are serious about their input, and how to follow up. As a result, they could clearly see that their input was not only listened to, but in many cases their input was implemented.

As far as a management tool, I have found it to be the only technique that really gets people involved, and it taps the best resource that any organization has—the brainpower of the whole organization—you solicit from everybody as much as you can—how they think, their best opinion, their best ideas, their best solutions. If you have five to ten people looking at a problem instead of one or two, you are going to receive a tremendous amount of information that you might otherwise overlook. This management approach is utilized for everything, from a new disciplinary policy to transfers to days off.

A key point, however, is that it is not a decision by the majority. Many times I accepted the majority recommendation because I felt that they were right; but there have been times when I have gone against the majority. I have the responsibility to make the final decision, and I may judge that a particular recommendation is not in the best interest of the department. But most of the time, the majority gives you good advice and a strong set of reasons why you should adopt their recommendation.

The approach is time consuming, but most decisions do not need to be made immediately. As a matter of fact, the worst decisions are the ones that are often made immediately. In fact, I have to admit, some mistakes in the past were due to making a decision too quickly. Afterwards when I think back if I had waited a few more days, I would have made a different decision. On the whole, you will find that if you have the time to look at the situation before you make the decision, you make better decisions. It is time consuming, but that is simply one of the trade-offs. Moreover, if people have a say, then they have an investment in the decision. Consequently, they will accept it more readily than if it is imposed on them.

My policy-making discretion varies. As head of my department I have considerable policy-making authority. Most policies that involve the operations of the department are instituted at my final decision; however, they are almost never undertaken without considerable review from the executive staff. Major policy decisions that involve significant changes in the organization or involve additional resources or have major impact on overall city operations must secure the approval of the city manager and/or council.

INNOVATIONS AND SUCCESSES

I did two things that I felt the department should have done many years ago. First, planning ahead is one of the most important functions that you are going to undertake as an administrator, regardless of where you work. We established a five-year plan and we upgrade it every year. We evaluate it, change it, or do whatever has to be done, but we always have a five-year plan in effect. Everybody knows the general direction that we should be going in, and we disseminate that five-year plan for everyone to understand.

Who develops the plan? We have a number of people involved in that process. Twice a year, in July and in January, I take my top advisors, the assistant chiefs and the majors, on a retreat to some hotel in the city, and we lock ourselves up for a day or a day and a half. We discuss all the major problems that need to be looked into for the coming year as well as the next five years. We make decisions about what our path should be. We cover all the important items that we think will affect us, everything from budget to salary raises to fringe benefits to disciplinary problems to policy changes, and so forth.

Secondly, it is very hard for people to criticize you if they know you personally—if they have had an opportunity to talk to you. So every month I do two things: I have a group of officers from all ranks, twenty-four or thirty of them from all over the department, invited to come up to my office. We meet for an hour and a half, just they and I to discuss whatever they want to discuss. If they have heard rumors or have complaints, this is a forum in which they raise the issues. Additionally, once a month I do the same thing with twenty-five representatives of the non-sworn staff.

Moreover, I supplement those meetings by going out to briefing stations. I have six briefing stations and twice a year I go to each station to meet with the officers before they hit the street. If I have some important issues to discuss with them, or they need to be brought up to date on an issue, I'll take thirty minutes and have a session with them. I have found these kinds of activities to be extremely valuable. People want an opportunity to tell you what they think; and as long as they have that opportunity, it facilitates communication. It is time consuming. I ask myself sometimes, "Why am I doing this? I know the work is stacking up in the office." But it is valuable, and I owe them the opportunity to know me, to see me, to hear from me about issues and plans, and to answer some of their questions.

There are a couple of successes that I would like to mention. First, I am constantly in touch with the Hispanic and black communities. One of the key things that I have focused on to improve the department is the increased recruitment of minorities and women. I am very committed to the diversification of the police department. When I joined the police department in 1960, there were 400 police officers and there were only about six Hispanic patrolmen. Given the size of the Hispanic population in Phoenix at that time, this figure was ridiculously low. We now have almost 200 Hispanic officers in the department out of 1,750. We went from about three or four blacks in the department to well over a hundred. At that time we only had one or two women who were actually police officers; now we have approximately 150 women in our department.

I gave minority recruitment top priority. I said, "I don't want excuses, I don't want barriers, I want results." This carried over to the promotional processes as well. We have minority supervisors on the oral board to make sure that everybody gets an equal chance. If there is a policewoman that is in the promotion process, then we have a woman supervisor on the oral board, even if I have to borrow one from another agency. I have had people from Los Angeles and San Diego come over to be part of our process if women and minorities were going through that kind of evaluation.

Another success is in the area of resource distribution. We knew our resources were not going to be of the volume we wanted, so we looked around for assistance from within the department. As a result, we "civilianized" a lot of police officer positions. I felt that we were spending too much money training people to be officers to have them sit at a desk and answer a phone. We also removed all of our officers who were dispatchers and civilianized those positions. That was probably the best move we have ever made, because the civilians turned out to be more effective than our officers as dispatchers. We civilianized over seventy-five positions in the last four years and put those officers back on the street where their training can be best utilized.

A third success was the infusion of computers into the department. We now have what we call computer-aided dispatching. There are terminals in every squad car that, through the computer system, can be used to check license plates, driver's licenses, stolen property, serial numbers, wanted persons, and stolen cars. All of the information is at the officer's fingertips. Now they do not have to stop at a phone and call in—and wait and wait and wait. Through our computer system, we are connected throughout the whole state and even nationally with the National Information Crime Center on wanted people. Computerization has saved us millions of dollars because we have not had to add more and more policemen to do some things best handled by technology. I am quite proud of these accomplishments.

I would like to believe that the successes are because of the young, dynamic new leadership that I brought to the department. I say I would like to believe that, however, my staff would disagree with that assessment. In 1980, the year I became chief, we had the highest crime rate in the history of the police department. The crime rate went down 32 percent in my first four years. I think it was because there was new enthusiasm that resulted when we switched directions. We got away from the old tradition of doing police work—responding after the fact. You get the call, the crime has been committed, you get there, you try to solve it. Hopefully, if you are lucky, you get there in time to apprehend the criminal. We switched gears. We still do traditional police work, but now we have taken a more proactive approach, particularly in the area of crime prevention. That is the key to reducing crime, especially with juveniles, so we put a lot of manpower, money, and time in the prevention aspect of fighting crime. We have gotten the community involved in crime fighting, as well, in a variety of ways. The involvement of citizens to help us was very important in turning the crime rate around.

Probably my biggest weakness as an administrator is I often do not want to say no. Consequently, I must be on a hundred committees and commissions. It seems I am always going to conferences. I am trying to correct that weakness by being more selective, only doing those things I feel can have the greatest impact and where it will do the best for the city of Phoenix or the best for the police department. I overextend myself and, consequently, I do not really give good, true service to whichever organizations I belong to. If you fragment your involvement in this way, you cheat them and you cheat yourself.

Withdrawing is not easy, though, because as I continue to be a police chief, I have met a lot of people and helped a lot of people in all walks of life. They feel comfortable in calling me and saying, "Hey, we sure would like for you to come to this thing," or "We need you for this," or "Could you be on this committee?" It is hard to say no, because you know those people and you know that they need your help, and it becomes difficult. I would say watch yourself in that respect, do get involved, but do not overextend yourself.

PREPARATION AND LESSONS LEARNED

Twenty years of police experience with the last ten years in middle management combined with a college education made me competitive for the police chief position. Also seeking responsibilities and opportunities that got me involved with people in different segments of the community gave me considerable experience in dealing with people problems. To be successful, you should be knowledgeable in the areas of your responsibilities and have the confidence that you can do the job. You should seek assistance and advice from those around you who have skills or knowledge in areas you are weak in, and get people involved in things you want accomplished. Don't ever forget your roots.

You need to be flexible, keep in tune with what is going on, and participate in changes that increase productivity, solve problems, or encourage progress. To be prepared for opportunities, you must stay actively involved and add to your personal skills.

COMMUNITY RELATIONSHIPS

Support from the majority community has evolved over a period of time, particularly as it has become understood that I have encouraged high standards of honesty and integrity. I try to be forthright and open. My approach and departmental improvements have led to a positive image in the majority community.

All of these factors have been of great value in minority communities, as well. In addition, I get strong minority support because I have taken an aggressive posture on recruitment and promotion of minorities on the police force, and because I have dealt harshly with violations of civil rights and mistreatment of minorities whenever it has been found. I have also benefitted from continued activity in minority affairs. I provide assistance and service to a variety of civic organizations, and my involvement has resulted in enhanced support for me and the department.

A couple years after I became police chief, several columnists in our local newspapers really took me on as a target. To this day I am trying to figure out what it was that I did wrong. It was not until one particular columnist left that I got feedback on why he hated police, particularly me. In one column he even compared me to a banana republic dictator; his racism was really beginning to show. There was the headline, and I took it to my lawyer and said, "I got him now!" He says, "No, you don't." But, I did not have to raise a finger, I did not have to do a thing. A group of minority people paid a visit to that newspaper and they said, "You know, Ruben Ortega may be an S.O.B. but he's our S.O.B." In essence they were saying: "Give the guy a chance and back off. If you want to take him on simply because he is a minority, then you have got to take on a hundred thousand people in the city." I had never felt more proud to be a Hispanic than that day when I received the message about what had happened. This kind of support translates into, "Do not let us down." You are going to be evaluated, you are going to be looked at very closely, and there are those out there waiting for us to stumble. The minute one of us in a position of responsibility makes a mistake, it will be headlines for days.

One of my strengths as police chief of the city of Phoenix is that over the last twenty-six years I have gained the support and the trust of the minority community. I know there are persons in this community who would like to see me brought down. There is no doubt about it. I see it almost every day. If you picked up the headlines in this morning's paper, it is there. You can read between the lines. But my real strength is the fact that these (minorities) people believe in me and I thank God for it. If my detractors really want to remove me, they are going to have a battle on their hands. I look at that as a source of strength, not one that I would abuse but certainly one that I think makes my job a lot easier.

The message that I would reiterate to you is: When you get there, just do not forget where you came from and do not forget that there are a lot of us out there who are seeking those opportunities. Nobody can increase those opportunities any faster than we can by making sure that we have not stopped our efforts in recruiting, that we continually strive to help other minorities make gains in their respective departments or professions. We still need a tremendous amount of assistance to get more minority people up there in those positions because if we start sliding, we will lose a lot more than we have gained.

From time to time, some problems between the department and the minority community have risen and created a degree of tension. But overall those problems were quickly resolved with no loss of positive relations between us. In most cases it strengthened the relationship because they acted as reminders that we must constantly be in contact on matters of mutual concern. Minority employee groups of our department continue to be very supportive of me and the administration.

As chief, of course, I do not take a major role as spokesperson for any group. I must maintain a position of servant and equal provider of service to all. Behind the scenes, however, I may give advice or make suggestions that may help alleviate problems or obstacles or aid in the accomplishment of positive issues or goals.

GOALS FOR THE MINORITY COMMUNITY

I have a strong commitment to affirmative action and that objective is one of the criteria upon which my performance appraisals are based. I volunteered for that. We have a program in Phoenix called "Performance Achievement Program." Raises are based on the goals that you set early in the year and how well you have accomplished those goals. One of the goals in my Performance Achievement Program is, for example, to exceed the number of minority officers that were hired the previous year. I pass that on to my administrators and that is part of their Performance Achievement Program. If they want to get paid the highest possible salary raise, then they best not fail in the area of affirmative action.

We also have a goal in the area of promotions. Particularly in the nonsworn positions where we have more latitude, hopefully a significant percentage throughout the year will be minority promotions. In the area of women employees, for example, we have created a women's committee to continuously review issues that pertain to women in the department. As I said earlier, one of the policies that I implemented right after I became chief was that in any promotional examination if there are any minority applicants, there will be at least one minority on the oral board—and that includes women. If we have women applying for a sergeant's or lieutenant's position, then I will obtain assistance from other police departments that have female captains or lieutenants to sit on our boards.

I put a top priority on affirmative action. I send two of my top black administrators on two or three trips a year—to different states that have black universities—to try to encourage a number of black graduates to consider Phoenix as their future home. We do not have to do that with Hispanics. We have a bigger base here. One of the problems that we have encountered is that when we find a Hispanic or a black that we think not only can meet the qualifications but has the desire to be a police officer, he/she is also in demand by private industry. We are fighting hard to bring more minority recruits into law enforcement because they are in such high demand. Because of the competition, when we hire, they are the best.

I give frequent talks in the community, in particular at high schools that have a significant number of minority students, to encourage students to seek careers in law enforcement—in the police department, in the probation department or in the court system. We are constantly trying to remind them that there are career opportunities in our department. We make minority recruitment one of our top priorities, and we try to practice what we preach.

It is critical that those minorities who have reached high levels of accomplishment or influence continue efforts for additional changes and to assist others to achieve. Probably for some time to come, there will be a role for protest politics, but never for violent action.

UNIQUE PROBLEMS/OPPORTUNITIES DUE TO MINORITY STATUS

I try to avoid the appearance or perception in my influence that my ethnic background is a motivator for the position I take. This is especially difficult in instances involving the minority community or the promotion or discipline of minority employees. However, on important issues involving minorities, being a high-ranking minority public official does allow for others to carefully consider my opinion or recommendation. Therefore, I am usually successful in having my recommendations adopted. Being a minority administrator has prompted numerous invitations to be part of activities that I may not have been otherwise involved in, particularly serving on important boards or commissions, both locally and nationally. These activities and contacts give me an opportunity to be influential in various areas.

9
Minority Administrators: Lessons from Practice

Albert K. Karnig and
Paula D. McClain

The preceding chapters have elicited valuable responses from the contributors. They have placed their administrative positions in the rich context of their communities and organizations and have outlined their administrative philosophies, preparation, strategies, goals, successes, and failures. In these discussions, individual orientations and perspectives have come to life. The contributors differ in many significant respects: two are women, the others are men; three are Hispanic, two are black, and one is Native American; three (Davis, Ortega, and Valdez) work in the communities in which they were raised, whereas the others were recruited to their posts from other cities. The contributors were drawn from varying types of organizations and from cities that diverge greatly in size and ethnic heterogeneity. They react to different types of influences, and while they all hold major positions with substantial authority, they play a diverse set of roles—ranging from partisan political administrator (Davis) to police chief (Greenberg and Ortega) to generalist city manager (Murray and Valdez) to director of a nonprofit health agency (Kauffman). Nevertheless, despite these differences, there are impressive and instructive similarities in the contributor's perspective, beliefs, and administrative strategies.

TRUSTEE ROLE

The chief commonality among our contributors, one which is both philosophical and applied in nature, is a *trustee relationship* to minority communities. This trustee relationship is not a part of their formal role responsibilities, but evolves from personal values and commitments which they brought to their positions. Wahlke et al. (1962), in examining the representational role of legislators, identified the trustee as a major role orientation. According to Wahlke, a trustee claims to follow personal convictions, principles, and the dictates of conscience as a basis for making decisions. The trustee attempts to persuade those who disagree rather than changing his or her perspective. The trustee's decisions are judgments based on an evaluation of the facts, understanding of the problem, and other information that others may not possess. Finally, the trustee is willing to accept the political consequences of his or her independent decision making, because of deeply held beliefs that the decisions and orientations are correct.[1]

Although this definition refers to representational roles of elected officials, parts of it describe the role each of these administrators has taken with respect to minority communities. The contributors were not elected, and thus are not trustees in the sense outlined by Wahlke et al. Moreover, the positions they hold define the scope of their authority and limit the areas in which a trustee role is possible. None was hired by the minority community, and, with the exception of Kauffman, none works exclusively for minority citizens. Yet all indicated that they personally felt a responsibility to make a difference by their presence. As minority administrators, they assumed a responsibility to promote equality and open career and hiring opportunities for minority group members. They have adopted *trustee relationships* in the sense that they have utilized their positions to make affirmative action a priority in their organizations.

Our contributors all have actively embarked on strategies intended to bring about organizational change which will be beneficial to minority communities. As discussed in chapter 1, position constraints limit what minority administrators are able to do, but they have developed deep personal commitments to the advancement of minorities and merged this emphasis into their formal administrative roles. They have made diversification of the work force a criterion to evaluate themselves, as well as their subordinates, and they have undertaken to transform employment and hiring rules to ensure more access to minority applicants.

THE "NEW PUBLIC ADMINISTRATOR"

Several decades ago, the discipline of public administration began to see that the rigid dichotomy between politics and administration could not be justified and began to reassess the role of the public administrator. After a search for new modes of representativeness, the concept of a "new public administration" evolved. While the term "new public

MINORITY ADMINISTRATORS

administration" is no longer fashionable, and though several related components have been rejected, there are various key elements which are now part of the accepted wisdom of administrative behavior. According to H. George Frederickson, a proponent of this new direction:

> The policy-administration dichotomy lacks an empirical warrant, for it is abundantly clear that administrators both execute and make policy. The policy-administration continuum is more accurate empirically but simply begs the question. New Public Administration attempts to answer it in this way: Administrators are not neutral. They should be committed to both good management and social equity as values, things to be achieved, or rationales.
>
> A fundamental commitment to social equity means that new Public Administration is anxiously engaged in change. Simply put, new Public Administration seeks to change those policies and structures that systematically inhibit social equity....
>
> A commitment to social equity not only involves the pursuit of change but attempts to find organizational and political forms which exhibit a capacity for continued flexibility or routinized change.[2]

In essence, this view sees administrators as change agents who should not be afraid to take a controversial political stance, when necessary, to advance social equity in their programs, processes, and policies. In many ways, the administrators contributing to this volume are prototypical of a new public administration.

PERSONAL BACKGROUND AND PREPARATION

The contributors share various background features. For example, they all have origins in less-affluent families and were introduced to the world of work early in their lives. Each scratched out an education despite various adversities, and each began a career at a low level—in an internship, as a foot patrol officer, as a grants writer, etc.—before ascending the career ladder. Of course, they also share status as minority group members in the United States and each has a strong accompanying sense of ethnic identity. They have experienced discrimination. However, despite a pervasive conviction that opportunities for minorities have only recently become open, they do not dwell on the topic of discrimination.

In general, the contributors believe that their initial rigors, adversities, and multicultural experiences fostered a better grasp of human problems and issues, sensitivity to suffering, and valuable insight into interpersonal relations—thus helping to assure that certain kinds of issues will be raised rather than overlooked. Early "hard knocks" are seen to have been advantageous because, once overcome, they help produce more confident, tough administrators who can better handle stress and pressure. Interestingly, however, despite emphasizing the worth of experience in the "school of life," there is a ubiquitous stress on education, as well. Each placed enormous value on securing degrees and continuing education through lectures, workshops, seminars, introduction to new technology, and general self-improvement.

The contributors were assiduous in preparing for their present positions. As noted, each rose through the ranks—or moved from community to community—to pursue career aspirations. Skills and experiences were important, but so too were the credentials that were obtained. A basic model is provided in the contributors' comments:

1. Target a goal and prepare for its achievement by securing skills and credentials in the educational arena.
2. Learn by closely observing productive and successful individuals with whom you work in order to develop both style and substance.
3. Honestly assess and admit weaknesses and then seek to overcome them with assistance and training if needed.
4. Take a chance on new career directions if opportunities open and potential exists.
5. Face adversity with self-confidence without allowing obstacles to blunt your goals.
6. Continue training through formal and informal education in order to remain on the cutting edge.

REASONS FOR BEING HIRED AND EXPECTATIONS

Historically, opportunities for advancement to the highest administrative posts have been closed to minorities. Overt and subtle forms of racism have had effects in curtailing minority skills and qualifications by limiting education, employment, and other opportunities. When minorities did overcome discrimination and were able to secure credentials appropriate for top-level positions, racism often barred the door. Events over the last few decades, suggested in the Foreword and Chapter 1, have led to greater opportunities and the elimination of most forms of overt discrimination. In addition, affirmative action, hiring goals, and community pressures have promoted opportunities for minorities. Nonetheless, many of the contributors were "firsts" in their positions. Indeed, both city managers and both police chiefs were the first minorities in their posts. Moreover, critical political events had to precede their appointments, for example, the shift to district elections, a more representative city council, and a new mayor in Charleston; a new city manager in Tucson who was willing to take a chance; and civil disturbances in Phoenix. In each case, while competence and ability were essential conditions, the need for minority perspectives, the critical symbolism of minority appointments, and the willingness to take political risks were necessary, too. In addition, especially to such high-level positions outside civil service ranks, personal chemistry and personality traits were of central importance in the appointing process.

As we have emphasized, each of the contributors feels a particular obligation to minorities. As Ruben Ortega commented: "Don't ever forget your roots." Sylvester Murray presented a particularly interesting linkage between this obligation and the expectations of appointing officials. As Murray remarked, if a minority is appointed to a key position, those doing the appointing know that they are selecting a minority; and they expect that person to do certain things differently. The selection is a commitment to affirmative action and for dealing with other minority issues. He contends that there will be disappointment if a minority official in a major position fails to deliver on the expectations by not appointing other minorities to key posts and otherwise not helping to deal with minority concerns. The perspectives of minority officials, then, must be different than those of nonminorities. If the benefits of the appointment of a minority are to be greater than simply to the person appointed, the minority official must make a difference to other minorities.

However, the expectations of appointing officials and of minority and majority communities may be sorely unrealistic. As Reuben Greenberg noted, some in Charleston thought his appointment would result in the total elimination of black crime, others felt that the police would suddenly go easy on black criminals, and yet others believed that no white would ever again be promoted in the police ranks. With respect to this last point, Joel Valdez noted that minority administrators are often placed in tenuous situations because if they select a coethnic it will be seen as favoritism, and if a coethnic is not selected it will be viewed as "selling out."

POSITIONS

The contributors all had complex, challenging, high-level posts with substantial discretion and influence. They deal from positions of authority in their own organizations, but often must live with the effects of federal cutbacks and the policies made at other governmental levels or jurisdictions, over which they have little control. Their high-level posts often receive considerable media attention; however, with minorities in their particular positions, media scrutiny becomes magnified and community interest is enhanced. The contributors tend to live in glass houses. Clearly, the nature of these positions—pressure-packed, outside the civil service system, and the focus of much attention—makes for great vulnerability. There is no tenure or job security. Each could be dismissed at any time and without substantial reason. As a result, the administrative roles require a great measure of responsiveness.

The contributors' remarks provide a composite picture of the care and feeding of superiors: First and foremost, it is essential to keep superiors well informed, with no surprises, so that there is no danger of a superior appearing foolish or being taken off guard. The what, when, where, etc., of events must be communicated in a timely fashion. Informal mechanisms, rather than public meetings, should be employed to answer questions and resolve differences of view. Trust and rapport are essential. Direct challenges and attacks are to be avoided. Influence is wrought through activities in which information, perspective, and expertise are supplied. Occasionally, there may be behind-the-scenes contacts with the press or influential parties to help set an agenda, plant ideas, or otherwise surface issues, though this approach is highly risky and cannot be employed frequently or indiscreetly.

The positions discussed in this volume are attractive in ways that only highly powerful offices can be. They offer remarkable opportunities to influence the course of public events and public outcomes. They can also take a profound toil on the personal lives of incumbents. Media and community attention, coupled with long hours and often stressful decisions, cuts sharply into time available for families and children. For some, at least, as Davis suggested, the career comes before "personal relations." The pressures of major decision-making positions have impact on the personal lives of nonminorities, as well. However, since minorities are expected to serve both as *officials* with normal duties, and as *minority officials* with symbolic and substantive responsibilities on various committees, task forces, etc., simply because they are minorities, the impact on minority officials is apt to be greater. Furthermore, the most severe effects on private lives are likely to be experienced by minority women, who carry both minority and women's obligations and also frequently suffer from traditional expectations to play female roles at home.

ADMINISTRATIVE PHILOSOPHIES, PROCESSES, AND STRATEGIES

Just as the contributors have strategies in dealing with supervisors, they also emphasize particular approaches in working with their subordinates and managing their organizations. Although computerization and automation are increasingly important for organizational success, as remarks by Ruben Ortega and Joel Valdez suggest, human beings remain the chief variables in determining the organization's effectiveness. While there are differences of nuance and occasionally of substance, as a whole several clear and consistent orientations about employee relationships emerge from the presentations found in the preceding chapters.

There is overall agreement that "flat" organizations are best, that is, those without rigid hierarchies. Though each is alert to avoiding end-runs around line officers, each also is readily available to employees in the organization and makes it a point routinely to sample employee views. Leadership and vision come from the top, of course, and the contributors all espouse both this view and the need to provide leadership in promoting excellence. Nonetheless, they also recognize that effective leadership requires extensive time devoted to listening and getting good advice from others. Murray suggested that management is "the effective manipulation of people and money." The stress, he said, is on the word "effective," as opposed to efficient or economical. The objective is a good outcome—one that you would like to see unfold. Motivation occurs by recognizing employees as individuals, seeking their input, and allowing them to influence policies and procedures.

The most desirable forms of motivation are rooted in trust, rapport, commitment, and loyalty. Interpersonal skills are indispensable but so too is clear communication and clear expectations. As a consequence, the contributors support the use of planning and management-by-objective approaches to focus on goals, establish accountability, and link both promotion and pay to performance rather than simply to seniority. An effective example of this approach is the Performance Achievement Program instituted by Police Chief Ortega in Phoenix. Moreover, as Greenberg commented, it is valuable to set accountability as high as possible in the organization to help assure that everyone is pulling together.

There is consensus on the importance of surrounding oneself with bright and candid colleagues who have expertise, getting necessary counsel and advice, and delegating responsibility. As Joel Valdez noted, it is also valuable to establish personal relationships with department heads and key staff members. Information, however, may come from myriad sources, and to help guarantee the free flow of information and perspective in both directions, the contributors support the usefulness of "management-by-walking around." Not merely does each meet routinely with staff and subordinates in order to manage, each seeks to address issues at the delivery level in order to develop sensitivity, trust, and better information. Such an approach, as Kauffman suggested, helps to eliminate isolation, loss of support, and bad decision making, as well as helping to create sensitivity to particular problems and issues at the delivery level.

A good illustration of effective motivation may be found in Kauffman's effort to secure accreditation from the Joint Commission for the Accreditation of Hospitals. By virtue of the processes she created, employees developed personal involvement in the outcome. By giving each employee an area of responsibility, everyone had the mission to serve as an advocate for achieving accreditation rather than resisting what would otherwise be a complex and arduous undertaking. The process, then, helped to promote a sense of commitment and an investment in the outcome.

Committee processes, what Ruben Ortega refers to as "team style" management, are heavily employed by each contributor, both to identify and discuss problems as well as to recommend the solutions. Participation tends to give committee members stakes in the eventual decisions, promotes collegiality, and helps to produce a sense of "team." Furthermore, consistent with this view concerning participatory management, the contributors use mechanisms by which rules and regulations, where possible, tend to be made at the lowest operational levels. In this fashion, responsibilities are linked to those actually performing duties; and solutions for problems are found by those who need issue resolution. The overall committee approach requires a delicate balance between accepting recommendations—so that participants feel that they are a part of the process and that their views are respected—and being willing to "bite the bullet" by rejecting recommendations that are not in the best interest of the organization. Greenberg called his process "democratic centralism." Not all contributors would use this term, initially coined by the revolutionary founder of the USSR, V. I. Lenin, but each would accept the basic premise: There should be broad and diverse participation in discussions and in the formulation of solutions to issues. However, once a decision is made, everyone—including those who disagree—must support the decision and seek to implement it effectively.

SUPPORT GROUPS

There are great differences and some interesting similarities in the groups which support the administrators contributing to this volume. Variations in group support are based on different roles played and differing personal approaches. Supporters range from labor unions and the political left to Rotary, chambers of commerce, and big business; from partisan to nonpartisan organizations; from self-help groups and issue-based associations to special interest business constituencies which compose important elements in the formal and informal structures of local power. In addition, however, without exception, there is strong support from minority associations, particularly those sharing the ethnicity of the administrator, e.g., black ministers and civil rights organizations working to support black administrators. Moreover, women's groups and networks are chief sources of support for women administrators, as well.

Support, of course, does not come without cost. To encourage and maintain such support, contributors must attend meetings of myriad organizations, wedge social functions into busy schedules, be available on relatively brief notice, and, at least on an overall level, demonstrate sensitivity to the issues and positions favored by support groups. In this sense, these administrators have parallels with their elective brethren. Bridges must be built and constituencies nurtured. Some of the relevant activities are nicely summarized by Kauffman: identifying a broad coalition of supporters—including the mayor's office, churches, labor, hospitals, minority agencies, etc.—developing public relations materials, stimulating interest on the part of the news media, and generally developing political support for her agency.

There is abundant variation in the degree to which minority administrators are visible members of minority organizations. Some are highly and openly involved. Others are not, but all are available and work behind the scenes to promote improvement in conditions for minorities. The contributors' comments make it clear that given the broad support received from minority communities, minority administrators have significant obligations. Nonetheless, in their activities and support of minority issues, there is general agreement that, as Davis said, one cannot wear being a minority on one's sleeve. Credibility will be quickly lost if minority administrators develop reputations for always adopting minority perspectives. However, much can be done directly and, as noted, work often is undertaken behind the scenes. In addition, influence over outcomes can be developed simply by knowing the issues better than others and in both the questions raised and the perspectives offered.

STRATEGIES TO IMPROVE MINORITY OUTCOMES

Earlier in this chapter, it was noted that all of the contributors assumed a "trustee" role with respect to minorities. As Davis said, "This role is expected by the minority community." Moreover, as Murray noted, the role was also expected by officials who appointed them. The trustee role, as articulated by those contributing to this volume, is predicated on a rather well-organized set of orientations. First and foremost, there is the view that minority administrators must make a difference in the leadership, service, and models they offer—that they must be more than just good administrators, since they have deep obligations to the minority community and must help to destroy counterproductive stereotypes. The chief goals are greater equality of outcomes and enhanced participation in decision-making processes. The following are among the key strategies most prominently mentioned:

- When appropriate, serve as spokesperson for minority communities, using knowledge, perspectives, and influence to produce policies and procedures favorable to more equitable outcomes.
- Work behind the scenes when necessary to seed, influence, and otherwise promote enlightened policies and to help resolve grievances.
- Serve as a community channel enhancing the access of minorities to decision makers, thereby reducing the gap between the access of minority and majority groups.
- Act as a valuable funnel of information concerning job opportunities, procurement specifications, and the like.
- Advertise widely and recruit personnel at minority institutions.
- Sensitize others to stereotypes about race.
- Maintain a current list of qualified minorities who can be recommended at short notice for service on boards and commissions to promote political representativeness.
- Work to secure minority participation in the appointment process by assuring that minorities serve on boards which recommend applicants.
- Assure that affirmative action is used in writing contracts.
- Identify other minorities in the organization and support them with opportunities and positive comments.
- Mentor and groom others in the organization by working closely with them, providing ample opportunities for development, encouraging skill development through training, and securing the types of positions that will help them develop professionally.
- Assure that minorities are on interview lists so that they will have an opportunity to be selected for open positions.
- Block employment decisions if they are discriminatory or poorly supported.
- Link affirmative action to merit raises and assign hiring officials specific targets.

There is no Pollyanna among the contributors. They are tough-minded administrators who fully understand that improvements for minorities will come only painstakingly. Equality and equitable participation at all levels of government—not only at the point of entry, but in top-level positions, as well—are not easy accomplishments. Such outcomes will require commitment, industriousness, assertiveness, and, as Davis put it, a "full court press" in diverse arenas. There are no shortcuts to influencing decisions and choices so that permanent change may follow. The contributors share a recognition, in addition, that equity will not be a simple consequence of government policy. Indeed, sometimes even apparently successful government approaches do not strike at the cause of problems, but, instead, deal with local symptoms. A good illustration of this situation is found in both Seattle and Charleston, where respective "neighborhood" centered approaches reduced homelessness, alcoholism, and crime, but resulted in a migration of specific problems because they did not treat the underlying "population" problems. To be sure, equal opportunity for education, training, and employment—in addition to effective monitoring to assure fair treatment—are essential conditions that have not yet been met. But there are responsibilities in minority communities, too. As Kauffman contends, minorities must be prepared before they assume roles as key decision makers because selection of underprepared minorities would result in the unwarranted continuation of debilitating stereotypes. Moreover, she suggests minorities must look closely at their own communities to identify destructive forces and to remedy them through their own actions. Honest assessments of the sources of problems must be combined with proactive strategies such as those outlined above if the nation is to witness increasing equality between minorities and the majority.

CONCLUSION

Minority administrators in the 1990s and into the twenty-first century will face a host of obstacles—from (hopefully diminishing) discrimination to suspicion that they are in their position simply because they are minorities, from a host of administrative tugs of war and issues that all administrators—majority or minority—must face, and from special minority concerns. In addition, since minority administrators disproportionately will be found in minority communities, they must wrestle disproportionately with poverty, disorder, and the panoply of problems and opportunities which arise in the inner city.

In his recent work, Herbert identified several managerial skills important for the minority administrator:

- An ability to operate effectively in conflict situations. The administrator must possess bargaining skills (so that he can deal both with citizens and employees and with elected officials and central staff personnel in resolving or preventing conflict).
- A familiarity with group dynamics. This means an ability to understand why and how groups are created and die; what they are attempting to accomplish; and how one might best work with them.
- An understanding of the feelings, demands, frustrations, and hopes of those citizens with whom he works.
- An ability to work in very tenuous, highly uncertain work situations where clear-cut solutions are difficult to define and environmental conditions are constantly changing....
- An ability to assume responsibility for all that goes along with making political decisions, and in a sense, share the policy-making function with elected officials.[3]

In Chapter 2, Henderson examined the challenges facing minority administrators in the 1990s. Among the key elements are: (1) accommodating urban socioeconomic needs in demographically changing cities; (2) reconciling personal, professional, advocacy, and other elements of their roles, i.e., maintaining role elasticity; (3) aligning their own agendas with those of elected officials; (4) managing public relations; (5) dealing with resource constraints; and (6) establishing and promoting productive interpersonal and intergroup relationships inside the bureaucracy and externally across the community.

The items offered by Herbert and Henderson constitute a formidable list of skills and orientations needed by minority administrators in meeting the challenges of the future. Contributors to this volume have all faced complex sets of issues and circumstances, and they have succeeded in putting theoretical principles into practice. Minority administrators in the 1990s, very much like those represented in this volume, will need to combine the traditional objectives of efficiency and productivity with newer emphases on social equity if they are to be successful in administering their organizations. We believe majority administrators must develop similar perspectives and skills. If the administrators in this volume are any guide, future minority administrators will emphasize trustee relationships with minority communities and attempt to promote minority participation and equality of outcomes. Only the future can answer whether minority administrators generally will be as successful as those whose comments were captured in this volume in dealing with dynamic and complex administrative challenges.

NOTES

1. John C. Wahlke, Heinz Eulau, William Buchanan, and LeRoy C. Ferguson, *The Legislative System* (New York: John Wiley and Sons, Inc., 1962), pp. 272–76.

2. H. George Frederickson, "Toward a New Public Administration," reprinted in Jay M. Shafritz and Albert C. Hyde, eds., *Classics of Public Administration* (Oak Park, Ill.: Moore Publishiing Company, Inc., 1978), pp. 392–93.

3. A. W. Herbert, "Management under Conditions of Decentralization and Citizen Participation Revisited," in Lawrence C. Howard, Lenneal J. Henderson, and Derly G. Hunt, eds., *Public Administration and Public Policy: A Minority Perspective* (Pittsburgh, Pa.: Public Policy Press, 1977), p. 129.

Selected Bibliography

Bardach, Eugene. *The Implementation Game*. Cambridge, Mass.: MIT Press, 1977.
Browning, Rufus P., Dale Rogers Marshall, and Davis H. Tabb. *Protest Is Not Enough*. Berkeley: University of California, 1984.
Campbell, D., and J. Feagin. "Black Politics in the South." *Journal of Politics* (February 1975): 129–59.
Cobb, Roger W., Jennie-Keith Ross, and Marc Howard Ross. "Agenda Building as a Comparative Process." *American Political Science Review* 70 (March 1976):126–38.
Cole, L. "Electing Blacks to Municipal Office." *Urban Affairs Quarterly* (December 1976):223–42.
Combs, Michael W., and John Gruhl. *Affirmative Action*. Jefferson, N.C.: McFarland & Co., 1986.
Dye, T. R., and James Resnick. "Political Power and City Jobs: Determinants of Minority Employment." *Social Science Quarterly* 62 (September 1981):475–86.
Dye, Thomas. *Understanding Public Policy*. 5th ed. Englewood Cliffs, N.J.: Prentice-Hall, 1986.
Eisinger, P. K. "Black Employment in Municipal Jobs: The Impact of Black Political Power." *American Political Science Review* 76 (June 1982):380–92.
———. *The Politics of Displacement: Racial and Ethnic Transition in Three Cities*. New York: Academic Press, 1980.
Estrada, Leobardo, Chris F. Garcia, Reynaldo F. Marcias, and Lionel Maldonado. "Chicanos in the United States: A History of Exploitation and Resistance." *Daedalus* 110 (Spring 1981):103–32.
Frederickson, H. George. "Toward a New Public Administration." Reprinted in Jay M. Shafritz and Albert C. Hyde, eds., *Classics of Public Administration*. Oak Park, Ill.: Moore Publishing Company, Inc., 1978.

Garcia, Chris F., and Rudolph O. de la Garza. *The Chicano Political Experience*. North Scituate, Mass.: Duxbury Press, 1977.

Gross, Neal, Ward Mason, and Alexander McEachern. *Exploration in Role Analysis*. New York: John Wiley and Sons, Inc., 1958.

Henderson, Lenneal J. "Administrative Advocacy and Black Urban Administrators." *The Annals* (September 1978):68–79.

———. *Administrative Advocacy: Black Administrators in Urban Bureaucracies*. Palo Alto, Calif.: R & E Research Associates, Inc., 1979.

———. "Beyond Equity: The Future of Minorities in Urban Management." *Public Management*, vol. 64, no. 6 (June 1982):2–3.

———. "Black Administrators and the Politics of Administrative Advocacy." In L. S. Yearwood, ed., *Black Organizations: Issues on Survival Techniques*. Lanham, Md.: University Press of America, 1980.

———. "Public Technology and the Metropolitan Ghetto." *The Black Scholar* (March 1974):9–17.

Herbert, A. W. "Management under Conditions of Decentralization and Citizen Participation Revisited." In Lawrence C. Howard, Lenneal J. Henderson, and Derly G. Hunt, eds. *Public Administration and Public Policy: A Minority Perspective*. Pittsburgh, Pa.: Public Policy Press, 1977.

———. "The Minority Administrator: Problems, Prospects, and Challenges." *Public Administration Review*, vol. 34, no. 6 (November/December 1974):556–63.

Holden, Matthew, Jr. *The Politics of the Black "Nation."* San Francisco: Chandler Publishing Co., 1973.

Horton, Raymond D. "Expenditures, Services, and Public Management." *Public Administration Review*, vol. 47, no. 5 (1987):378.

Howard, Lawrence C., Lenneal J. Henderson, and Daryl Hunt, eds. *Public Administration and Public Policy: A Minority Perspective*. Pittsburgh, Pa.: Public Policy Press, 1977.

Howard, Lawrence C., and Deryl Hunt. "Black Administrators in Urban Bureaucracy." *The Journal of Afro-American Issues*, vol. 3, no. 2 (Spring 1975):130–42.

Huddleston, Mark W. *The Public Administration Workbook*. New York: Longman, 1987.

Jones, M. "Black Officeholders in Local Governments of the South." *Politics* (March 1973):49–72.

Karnig, Albert K. "Black Representation on City Councils." *Urban Affairs Quarterly* (December 1976):223–42.

Karnig, Albert K., and Paula D. McClain. "The New South and Black Economic and Political Development." *The Western Political Quarterly* (December 1985):539–50.

Kearney, Richard C., and Chandan Sinha. "Professionalism and Bureaucratic Responsiveness: Conflict or Compatibility." *Public Administration Review*, vol. 48, no. 1 (January/February 1988):571.

Keech, William J. *The Impact of Negro Voting*. Chicago: Rand McNally, 1968.

Krislov, Samuel. *Representative Bureaucracy*. Englewood Cliffs, N.J.: Prentice-Hall, 1974.

Lipsky, Michael. *Protest in City Politics*. Chicago: Rand McNally, 1970.

SELECTED BIBLIOGRAPHY

Lynn, Laurence E., Jr. *Managing Public Policy*. Glenview, Ill.: Scott, Foresman Company, 1987.

Maniha, John K. "Structural Supports for the Development of Professionalism Among Police Administrators." *Pacific Sociological Review*, vol. 16, no. 3 (July 1973):317.

Meier, Kenneth John. "Representative Bureaucracy: An Empirical Analysis." *The American Political Science Review*, vol. 69, no. 2 (June 1975):526–42.

"Metro U.S.A. Data Sheet." *Population Today*, vol. 15, no. 12 (December 1987).

Monteih, Richard. "Placement in Action." *Public Management*, vol. 57, no. 11 (November 1975):3.

Moore, Joan, and Henry Pachon. *Hispanics in the United States*. Englewood Cliffs, N.J.: Prentice-Hall, 1985.

Nagel, Joane. "The Political Mobilization of Native Americans." *The Social Science Journal* 19 (July 1982):37–45.

Nelson, William E., and Philip J. Meranto. *Electing Black Mayors*. Columbus: Ohio State University Press, 1977.

Pressman, Jeffrey, and Aaron Wildavsky. *Implementation*. Berkeley: University of California Press, 1973.

Robinson, Rose. "The Conference of Minority Public Administrators." *Public Administration Review*, vol. 34, no. 6 (November/December 1974):552.

Rodgers, Harrell R. "Fair Employment Laws for Minorities: An Evaluation of Federal Implementation." In Charles S. Bullock, III, and Charles M. Lamb, eds., *Implementation of Civil Rights Policy*. Monterey, Calif.: Brooks/Cole Publishing Co., 1984.

Sabatier, P., and D. Mazmanian. "The Implementation of Public Policy: Framework of Analysis." *Policy Studies Journal* 8 (special issue no. 2, 1980):445–88.

Saltzstein, Grace H. "Female Mayors and Women in Municipal Jobs." *American Journal of Political Science* 30 (February 1986):140–64.

Sanders, Charles L. *Black Professionals' Perceptions of Institutional Racism in Health and Welfare Organizations*. Fairlawn, N.J.: R. E. Burdick, Inc., 1973.

U.S. Commission on Civil Rights. *For All the People, By All the People*. Washington, D.C.: U.S. Government Printing Office, 1969.

Van Horn, Carl. *Policy Implementation in the Federal System*. Lexington, Mass.: D. C. Heath, 1979.

Van Meter, D. S., and C. E. Van Horn. "The Policy Implementation Process: A Conceptual Framework." *Administration and Society* (February 1975):538–60.

Wahlke, John C., Heinz Eulau, William Buchanan, and LeRoy C. Ferguson. *The Legislative System*. New York: John Wiley and Sons, Inc., 1962.

Welch, Susan, and Albert K. Karnig. "The Impact of Black Elected Officials on Urban Expenditures and Intergovernmental Revenues." In D. R. Marshall, ed., *Urban Policy Making*. Beverly Hills, Calif.: Sage, 1979.

Index

Administrative advocacy, 5, 20–26, 28–30
Administrative failures, 45, 81, 97
Administrative philosophy, 41–43, 60, 79–80, 94–118, 134–36
Administrative strengths, 47, 85–86, 140
Administrative successes, 43–45, 61–62, 81, 97, 121–23, 137–38
Administrative weaknesses, 86, 97, 138
Affirmative action, 5–6, 19, 24, 53–54, 101, 125–27, 140–41, 146
Agenda setting, 2
American Indian Movement (AIM), 3
American Indians, mobilization of, 3
American Society for Public Administration (ASPA), 26, 61, 73
Arizona, 2
Arizona State University, School of Public Affairs, 86
Asians, in Los Angeles, 33
Atlanta, Georgia, 4

Baltimore, Maryland, 132
Bay of Pigs, 3

Birmingham, Alabama, 4
Blacks: mayors, 4; mobilization of, 1–2; political representation, 4–5
Bradley, Tom, 33, 43, 46
Brown, Lee, 109
Budgets, 36, 92, 95
Bureau of Indian Affairs, 3

California, 2, 131
Carter, Jimmy, 39
Castro, Fidel, 3
Charleston, South Carolina, 107–11
Chavez, Cesar, 55
Chicago, Illinois, 4, 132
Chicano movement, 2
Cisneros, Henry, 4
City managers, number of minority, 5
Civil Rights Act of 1964, 2, 19, 63
Civil rights movement, 1–2
Cleveland, Ohio, 4
Cobb, Roger W., 2
Colorado, 2
Community Development Block Grant, 44
Community relationships, 48–52, 71–

73, 86–88, 100–103, 111, 125–28, 139–40
Conference of Minority Public Administrators (COMPA), 27, 61
Cuba, 3
Cubans, 3

Democratic centralism, 116, 150
Denver, Colorado, 4
Detroit, Michigan, 4, 132

Economic Opportunity Act, 24
Effective manipulation, 60, 149
Elected officials, minority, 5
El Partido de La Raza Unida, 2
Equal Employment Opportunity Act of 1972, 5, 19
Equal Employment Opportunity Commission, 5

Ferrer, Maurice, 4
Flat organizations, 149
Florida, 3

Gary, Indiana, 4
Goals, minority community, 52–55, 73–74, 89, 103, 128–29, 140–41
Gonzales, Larry, 51
Gramm-Rudman-Hollings, 44, 54, 93
Great Society Program, 24

Harvard University, 99
Hatcher, Richard, 4
Henderson, Lenneal J., 6, 20
Herbert, Adam W., 8, 10, 16, 19, 20, 26, 28, 153
Hickey, Norman, 66
Hispanics, mobilization of, 2–3; Cubans, 3; mayors, 4; Mexican Americans, 2; political representation, 4; Puerto Ricans, 2, 3, 4
Holden, Matthew, Jr., 5, 7, 10, 16, 29
Horizontal affirmative action, 127
Horton, Raymond D., 15
Houston, Texas, 109, 132

Implementation, policy, 4–5, 15
Innovations, 43–45, 60–62, 80–81, 95–97, 118–23, 136–38

International Personnel Management Association (IPMA), 26

Johnson, Lyndon, 3
Joint Center for Political Studies, 4
Joint Commission for the Accreditation of Hospitals (JCAH), 80, 149

King, Martin Luther, Jr., 2, 55, 63

League of United Latin American Citizens (LULAC), 24
Lessons learned, 45–48, 62–71, 81–86, 97–100, 123–25, 138–39
Lipsky, Michael, 2
Long, Norton, 7
Los Angeles, California, 4, 33–58

Management by objectives, 41
Management by Wandering Around (MBWA), 79, 149
Maniha, John K., 25–26
Manpower Development and Training Act (MDTA), 24
Mazmanian, Daniel, 4
Means, Russell, 3
Meese, Edwin, 59
Mentoring, 70, 152
Mexican Americans, 2
Miami, Florida, 4
Minority administrators: demands on, 8–9; dilemmas, 9; future skills, 153–54; importance of, 4–6; role elasticity, 15–16
Minority Executive Director's Coalition (MEDC), 87
Model cities, 24
Movimento Estudiantil Chicano de Aztlan (MECHA), 2

National Association of Black Lawyers, 27
National Association of Black Psychologists, 27
National Association of Black Social Workers (NABSW), 27
National Association of Health Service Executives, 27

INDEX

National Association of Hispanic Elected Officials, 27
National Forum of Black Public Administrators, 27
New Mexico, 2
New Orleans, Louisiana, 4
New York City, 3, 131, 132
Northwestern University, 99

Open Housing Act of 1968, 2
Operation PUSH, 24

Peña, Frederico, 4
Pendleton, Clarence, 39, 59
Performance Achievement Program, 140, 149
Philadelphia, Pennsylvania, 4
Phoenix, Arizona, 131–42
Pima Community College, 100
Policy-administration dichotomy, 145
Portillo, Lopez, 39
Preparation for responsibilities, 45–48, 62–71, 81–86, 97–100, 123–25, 138–39
Public administration, 41, 46, 144
Public administrators, 4, 5, 15, 47
Puerto Ricans, 2, 3, 4

Remy, Ray, 42
Representative bureaucracy, 4, 5, 6, 7, 20
Role, constraints, 6, 7; elasticity, 15, 16, 29; model, 38–39

Sabatier, Paul, 4
San Antonio, Texas, 4
San Diego, California, 59
Seattle, Washington, 75–90
Seattle Indian Health Board, 75–77
Social equity, 145
Stanford University, 99
Stokes, Carl, 4
Support group, 150

Team management, 134, 150
Texas, 2
Torres, Art, 51
Trustee relationship, 143, 151
Tucson, Arizona, 91–105

United Mexican Students (UMAs), 2
University of Arizona, 100
University of California at Los Angeles, 51, 99
University of Michigan, 99
University of Pennsylvania, 62
Urban League Opportunities Industrialization Center, 24
U.S. Commission on Civil Rights, 17, 59

Van Horn, Carl, 4
Van Meter, Carl, 4
Voting Rights Act of 1965, 2, 5

Wahlke, John, 144
Washington, D.C., 132
Wharton School of Finance, 62, 99

About the Contributors

JULIAN BOND is a former Georgia state senator and noted civil rights activist and lecturer. He is presently an adjunct professor of political science at Drexel University. Senator Bond was first elected to a seat in the Georgia House of Representatives in 1965, but was prevented from taking office in January 1966 by members of the legislature who objected to his statements about the war in Vietnam. After winning a second election in February 1966, he was once again denied membership in the legislature. He won a third election in November 1966, and in December 1966 the United States Supreme Court ruled unanimously that the Georgia House had erred in refusing him his seat. On January 9, 1967, he took the oath of office and became a member of the Georgia House of Representatives and in 1974 was elected to the State Senate. He served in the Senate until 1986 when he unsuccessfully ran for the U.S. Congress. Senator Bond is president of the Atlanta chapter of the NAACP and is president emeritus of the Southern Poverty Law Center. Senator Bond, a noted poet, is a graduate of Moorehouse College.

GRACE MONTAÑEZ DAVIS is deputy mayor of the city of Los Angeles, a position she was appointed to in 1975 by Mayor Tom Bradley. Although a noted public figure, Davis holds a B.A. in Chemistry and a master's degree in microbiology from the University of California at Los Angeles, distinguishing herself in the field of cancer research. She first entered public life in 1964 as administrative assistant to Congressman George E. Brown, Jr. From 1966 to 1973 Davis was a manpower development specialist with the U.S. Department of Labor. In 1973, Mayor Bradley recruited her to become the director of human resources for the office of the mayor, a position she held until her elevation to deputy mayor.

REUBEN M. GREENBERG is chief of police of Charleston, South Carolina, having been appointed in 1982. He was formerly the undersheriff of the San Francisco County Sheriff's Department; a major with the Savannah, Georgia Police Department; chief of police in Opa-Locka, Florida; chief deputy sheriff of Orange County, Florida Sheriff's Department; and a deputy director of the Florida Department of Law Enforcement. He received a B.A. degree from San Francisco State University in 1967, a master's degree in public administration from the University of California, Berkeley in 1969; and a master's degree in city planning also from Berkeley in 1975. He was assistant professor of sociology at California State University, and has taught political science at the University of North Carolina at Chapel Hill, and criminal justice at Florida International University.

LENNEAL J. HENDERSON is currently head and professor, department of political science, and director of the Bureau of Public Administration at the University of Tennessee at Knoxville. He was formerly a professor in the School of Business and Public Administration at Howard University (1979–87); a Ford Foundation, National Research Council, Postdoctoral Fellow at the Johns Hopkins School of Advanced International Studies in Washington, D.C.; a policy analyst in the U.S. Department of Energy; and associate director of research at the Joint Center for Political Studies in Washington, D.C. He has served as chairman of the Mayor's Advisory Committee on Resources and Budget for the District of Columbia; chairman of the Citizens' Energy Advisory Committee for the District of Columbia (1981–87); as a member of the Mayor's Council of Economic Advisors; and a member of the Mayor's Block Grant Advisory Committee for the District of Columbia. He received his A.B., M.A., and Ph.D. degrees in political science from the University of California at Berkeley. He has authored or edited four books and numerous articles.

JOANN KAUFFMAN is executive director of the Seattle Indian Health Board. Prior to her appointment in 1982, she was the director of the Northern Idaho Indian Health Board, a position she held from 1979 to 1982. Kauffman has also worked as a public health advisor for the U.S. Public Health Service; a resource developer for the Seattle Indian Health Board from 1975–77; and acting director of American Indian Mental Health. She received her Bachelor of Arts degree in human services planning from Western Washington University, and a Master of Public

ABOUT THE CONTRIBUTORS

Health degree from the University of California at Berkeley. She is a member of numerous professional associations and boards and commissions.

SYLVESTER MURRAY, former city manager of San Diego, is a management consultant with Coopers Lybrand of Columbus, Ohio. Prior to being appointed city manager of San Diego, Mr. Murray served as city manager of Cincinnati, Ohio (1979–85); Ann Arbor, Michigan (1973–79); and Inkster, Michigan (1970–73). From 1969 to 1970 he served as assistant city manager of Richland, Washington, and was assistant to the city manager of Daytona Beach, Florida from 1964 to 1969. Mr. Murray holds a Bachelor of Arts in history from Lincoln University, a Master of Governmental Administration from the Wharton School, Fels Institute, University of Pennsylvania; and a Master of Arts in economics from Eastern Michigan University.

RUBEN B. ORTEGA is chief of police of Phoenix, Arizona, having been appointed in 1980. A native of Glendale, Arizona, he is a 27½-year veteran of the Phoenix Police Department, having worked most major aspects of police assignments including patrol and detective in vice, narcotics, criminal investigations, and community relations. While progressing through the ranks of the Phoenix Police Department, he taught throughout the state on police-community relations. Chief Ortega is a graduate of Phoenix College and Northern Arizona State University, where he received his B.S. degree in police science and administration. Among numerous memberships on boards and organizations, he has been a member of the executive committee of the International Association of Chiefs of Police, the Police Executive Research Forum, the U.S. Attorney General's Task Force on Family Violence, the Arizona Criminal Justice Commission, the Commission on Accreditation for Law Enforcement Agencies, and he is a graduate of the FBI National Executive Institute.

JOEL VALDEZ has been city manager of Tucson since 1974. A native Tucsonian, Mr. Valdez served previously as assistant city manager from 1971 to 1974; administrative assistant for the city from 1966 to 1971; and an administrator of detention services for Pima County government from 1958 to 1966. He serves on numerous national boards including the National Academy of Public Administration, the American Society for Public Administration, the International City Management Association, and the White House Conference on Balanced National Growth and Economic Development. Mr. Valdez received his Bachelor of Science degree in education from the University of Arizona and has attended executive seminars at Harvard University and MIT.

ABOUT THE EDITORS

ALBERT K. KARNIG is Provost and Vice President for Academic and Student Affairs at The University of Wyoming. He was formerly associate vice president for academic affairs and professor of public affairs at Arizona State University. He holds a Ph.D. in political science from the University of Illinois at Urbana. His research interests are in the areas of urban politics and policy and minority politics and policy. He is the co-author of *Black Representation and Public Policy Impact in American Cities* (with Susan Welch), and numerous articles and technical reports. His articles have appeared in numerous journals including *The Western Political Quarterly, Urban Affairs Quarterly, American Politics Quarterly, Women and Politics, Social Forces,* and *Journal of Politics.* He has served on the editorial boards of *American Politics Quarterly, Women and Politics,* and *Social Science Quarterly.*

PAULA D. MCCLAIN is associate professor of public affairs and director, Division of Policy Analysts and Evaluation, Center for Urban Studies at Arizona State University. She holds a Ph.D. in political science from Howard University and completed a postdoctoral fellowship at the Wharton School of the University of Pennsylvania. Her research interests are in the areas of urban homicide, gun regulation, and black and Hispanic political progress. She is the author of *Alienation and Resistance: The Political Behavior of Afro-Americans,* and co-author of *Black Homicide in an Environment of Urban Growth and Decline* (with Harold M. Rose). Her publications have appeared in numerous journals including *Policy Studies Review, Western Political Quarterly, Law and Policy Quarterly, The Journal of Environmental Systems,* and *Journal of Criminal Justice.* She is president-elect of the National Conference of Black Political Scientists and a former member of the Executive Council of the American Political Science Association. She is also literature review editor of *Policy Studies Review,* book review editor of the *National Political Science Review,* and co-editor of *Policy Studies Booknotes.*